"The same Chain that passes around the Slave's neck is fastened to the White Man's heel." Par. XXVII.

LEAVEN FOR DOUGHFACES;

OR

THREESCORE AND TEN PARABLES

TOUCHING SLAVERY.

BY

A FORMER RESIDENT OF THE SOUTH.

WE must suggest the People, in what hatred
This Power doth hold them; that to its sway, it would
Have made them mules, silenced their pleaders, and
Dispropertied their freedoms: holding them
In human action and capacity,
Of no more soul, nor fitness for the world,
Than camels in their war; who have their provand
Only for bearing burdens, and sore blows
For sinking under them.

Coriolanus mutat. mutand.

CINCINNATI:
BANGS AND COMPANY.
LONGLEY BROTHERS, 168½ VINE ST.
CLEVELAND: L. E. BARNARD & CO.
1856.

PREFACE.

If the author of this book shall in any manner contribute to bring about a rising among that patriotic class of the community for whose benefit it was produced, he will consider himself amply repaid for his labor. American *dough* being naturally heavy, he found it necessary to give as much pungency and strength to the leaven for it, as it could well bear. May the dough rise!

CONTENTS.

I.

THE THOUGHTFUL FREEMAN.

Slavery established in a community makes Free Laborers poor...... 13

II.

THE GREAT ROBBERY.

The Slave Power never keeps its Promises....................... 16

III.

THE STONES CRYING OUT.

That Nation which boasts most of its Liberty, is of all Nations most disgraced by its failure to secure it......................... 20

IV.

THE PEOPLE BECOME SOVEREIGN

A community exercises Popular Sovereignty, when it is governed by Slaveholders against its will.............................. 22

V.

THE CHIEF MAGISTRATE AND THE CHURCH DEPUTIES.

A part of the American Church is indifferent to the existence of Slavery, and a part devoted to it.......................... 24

VI.

THE COLONIZERS.

The main obstacle to the Colonization of the African American is his bondage.. 28

VII.

THE UNHAPPY FREEMAN.

The Southern Non-Slaveholder expects the Northern Freeman to do his duty.. 32

VIII.

THE CONGRESS OF REPUBLICS.

The Slaveholders wish to render Slavery more secure, when they extend the area of Freedom. 35

IX.

THE ORDER OF IGNORAMI.

It is hard to be a Know-Nothing and not be subservient to the Slave Power. 38

X.

THE DANGEROUS WOMAN.

Even a Woman who teaches Slaves to read, is a terror to their Masters. 42

XI.

THE HAPPY CANDIDATES.

Pleasant is the union between Doughface and Slaveholder when the People are to be cheated. 47

XII.

THE TRIAL OF THE LION'S SKIN.

The reputation of a Dead Hero cannot well be made to cover two Candidates for office. 52

XIII.

THE CHRISTIAN SLAVE.

Good Christians sell better than any other class of Slaves in the South. 57

XIV.

THE STRONG ASS.

The North is a strong Ass bowing between two burdens. 60

XV.

THE SLAVEHOLDER ENSLAVED.

It is right for a Slave to run away from his Master. 64

XVI.

THE LYING SLAVE.

If Slaves are Liars their Masters make them so. 69

XVII.

FREE TRADE.

Slaveholders desire to cripple the growth of the People. 72

XVIII.

THE DANGEROUS MAN.

In half the Union, it is unsafe for a Freeman to avow sentiments hostile to Slavery.......... 76

XIX.

THE APOSTLE OF LIBERTY.

Lying for Slavery is so well done by native Americans, that Irish Apostles find it an unprofitable business.......... 81

XX.

THE SLAVE-PEN.

There should ever be a Slave-Pen within sight of the Capitol to remind Aliens of the quality of American Liberty.......... 85

XXI.

THE WEIGHING OF THE MERITS.

Our Presidents are the tools of the Slave Power.......... 88

XXII.

THE DEMOCRAT ON A HUNT.

The latest Democracy finds a genial occupation in the chase of Fugitive Slaves.......... 90

XXIII.

THE BLACK EMBASSADORS.

The Ministers of Colored Nations cannot be received by the Government of the Union.......... 93

XXIV.

THE OPENING OF THE SEALS.

When the People bargain with Slaveholders, they ever get cheated. 96

XXV.

THE REJECTED OFFER.

A Fugitive Slave knows when he is happy as well as a born Democrat.......... 100

XXVI.

THE RULER OF A FREE PEOPLE TRIED.

The Chief Magistrate of a Free People needs not necessarily be a man.......... 104

XXVII.

THE SLAVE-HOLDER'S PROTECTION.

A body of ignorant Non-Slaveholding Freemen support the tyranny of the Slaveholders, and degrade themselves. 109

XXVIII.

THE CRACKED LIBERTY-BELL.

The cracked Bell which announced the signing of the Declaration of Independence, is the symbol of our National Freedom. 114

XXIX

THE RIGHT VICTIM.

The Fugitive Law enforced on a Democrat makes a man of him. 117

XXX.

THE POLITIC SLAVEHOLDERS.

The dread of Disunion, and the cry of Democracy, are the means with which the Slave Power subdues the People. 120

XXXI.

THE TRAITOR TO THE UNION.

Hostility to Slavery is treason to the Union. 123

XXXII.

THE INGENIOUS JUDGE.

It is only in a Republic that the Writ of Habeus Corpus can be used to recover Fugitive Slaves. 126

XXXIII.

THE PROTECTION OF LAW.

Citizens of a Free State barely suspected of aiding the escape of Fugitive Slaves may be sent to Prison in a Slave State. 129

XXXIV.

THE DOUGHFACE'S LETTER.

Hospitality costs nothing, when the toil of Slaves pays the expense. 132

XXXV.

THE KITCHEN SLAVE.

Not every Southern Gentleman dares to bring all his Children into the Parlor. 137

XXXVI.

THE PRESIDENTIAL CATECHISM.

A Democratic Candidate for the Presidency should aim to establish and perpetuate Slavery as a National Institution. 141

XXXVII.

THE REVIVAL IN THE SOUTH.

In the South there are two Gospels preached; one for the Master, and the other for the Slave. 146

XXXVIII.

THE SORE THROAT.

Democratic Senators do not prosper by speaking the Truth. 151

XXXXIX.

THE DOUGHFACE APPROVED

The Doughface aspires to nothing higher than the approbation of a Slaveholder. 154

XL.

THE PURIFIED MAIL BAGS.

The passage of Anti-Slavery papers through a Slave State is dangerous to free institutions. 161

XLI.

THE DISTRESSED SEMINARY.

Slaves may be sold to support the Gospel. 165

XLII.

THE RESTITUTION.

The Union will indemnify the Slaveholder against the loss of unborn Slave Babies. 169

XLIII.

THE DOUGHFACE RELIEVED.

American Democracy prefers Involuntary to Voluntary Amalgamation. 173

XLIV.

THE CAPTURED FUGITIVE AND THE MINISTERS.

A Clergyman in regular standing in the Chnrches cannot pray publicly for the freedom of a Fugitive Slave. 177

XLV.

THE FUGITIVE CHURCH-MEMBER.

In the South Church-members will run away from the means of grace. 180

XLVI.

THE EMANCIPATED DOUGHFACE.

Even a Doughface might become a lover of liberty, if made a Slave himself. 183

XLVII.

THE ORGAN FOR COLORS.

Slaveholders feel no repugnance to Amalgamation. 188

XLVIII.

THE PROSPECTS OF THE WOULD-BE CANDIDATES.

Whoever would be a Democratic President should not be an open advocate of Universal Liberty, neither should he do too much or too little for Slavery. 192

XLIX.

THE PRESIDENT ELECT.

Slavery makes so very small men Presidents, that most of them are amazed at their own success. 198

L.

THE POLYGAMOUS STATE.

Polygamy should not exclude a people from admission to the Union, when half the States practice it. 201

LI.

THE MUTTERING THUNDER.

The fear of Northern bayonets keeps the Southern Slave in subjection. 206

LII.

THE SURE SAFEGUARD.

The Slaveholder relies on the North as a last resort for protection against the insurrection of his Slaves. 210

LIII.

THE CABINET COUNCIL.

The greatest perplexity of American Presidents and their Cabinets arises from a desire to strangle the Liberty of the People. 215

LIV.

THE INSURRECTION.

Resistance to Tyrants is obedience to God. 219

LV.
THE NATIONAL GLORY.
National Glory consists in the possession of a Sound Democracy, a series of Democratic Presidents, and a laboring class of Slaves governed by a corps of Slaveholders. 222

LVI.
THE CHIEF MAGISTRATE ENTRANCED.
When a Pro-Slavery President speaks the truth, he is in an abnormal condition. 228

LVII.
THE UNEXPECTED PROPHECY.
The Slaveholders are not the South. 233

LVIII.
THE PATRIOT'S PORTRAIT.
American Statesmen are expected not so much to love liberty, as to profess a love for it. 237

LIX.
THE BESOTTED ALIEN.
The Alien who would ostracise the native Colored Man, should not be surprised to find himself ostracised by the native White. 242

LX.
THE BORDER RUFFIANS.
The Border Ruffians reside in Washington. 248

LXI.
THE YOUNG STATESMAN.
The Cowardice of the North is the Strength of the South. 253

LXII.
THE DANGEROUS PRIVILEGE.
Colored persons should not be allowed to testify against Whites, in cases of Church Discipline. 258

LXIII.
THE INWARD MESSAGE.
The Messages of our Democratic Presidents have an inner sense when they treat of Slavery. 263

LXIV.
THE UNSHACKLED FREEMAN.
Desert your Party when your Party deserts its Principles. 292

LXV.
THE CHOSEN MONUMENTS.
The Monuments to our Presidents should commemorate the deeds for which they are most distinguished. 295

LXVI.
THE DOUBLE TETE-A-TETE.
The Northern Doughface and Southern Slaveholder are equally fearful of Disunion. 299

LXVII.
THE STATESMAN IN HADES.
Pro-Slavery Statesmen fare no better in Hades than common sinners. 306

LXVIII.
THE UNKNOWN FUGITIVE.
Even the Church will sometime learn that Slavery is wrong. 309

LXIX.
THE QUALIFIED CITIZEN.
Only he who owns a Slave is entitled to Citizenship in the Territories of the Union. 313

LXX.
THE STRICKEN SENATOR.
Free Speech cannot be tolerated in Congress. 320

DEMOCRATIC STATUTE IN FORCE IN KANSAS, July 4, 1856.
Be it enacted by the Governor and Legislative Assembly of the Territory of Kansas, as follows: 329

LEAVEN FOR DOUGHFACES.

I.

THE THOUGHTFUL FREEMAN.

Slavery established in a community makes Free Laborers poor.

In a country where the greater part of the land was possessed by Slaveholders, there lived a freeman who knew no other occupation than the tilling of the soil. For his father had been poor, and unable to educate his son in any of the mechanic arts, or for any learned profession, needing his assistance in his own toil. Thus the son grew to manhood a cultivator of the ground, and going out free from his father's house, he cast about for the means of obtaining a livelihood. As there was no other resource for him, he rented a small patch of a slaveholder's plantation and settled upon it with his family. Unable to draw from it enough for a comfortable subsistence, he was wont to go abroad in quest of employment. Little, however, could he find to do; for on every plantation he was told that the slaves performed all the necessary labor, and that if he were hired he could receive but a pittance, as the slaves worked for nothing. Thus he was compelled to pass many a day in idleness, or in labor which brought him but a trifling income. So he resorted to hunting and fishing, and lived as he could. And the poorer and more destitute he became, the more did he grow ashamed of labor, because he dreaded to be put on a level with slaves. And, indeed, the very slaves laughed to see a freeman reduced to toil with themselves. Thus a great hatred grew up between him and them, and he rejoiced to see them in bondage, and they were delighted to see him degraded by poverty.

Now when his prospects were darkest for any relief, sitting one day in a gloomy mood in the door of his cabin, a slave accosted him, and asked the reason of his despondency. The freeman answered, that he had no certain means of subsistence, and could nowhere find labor to perform. Then said the slave: If you poor freemen would act wisely toward us who are slaves, you would soon cease to be poor. For how can you toiling non-slaveholders expect to be *paid* for your labor, when *we slaves* are compelled to do the same labor *for nothing*. Liberate us, you poor freemen, from bondage, and we will liberate you. For when we can charge a price for our work, then *all* needful labor will bring a price, and you will always be able to find employment, and will live comfortably. But it is certain, that if we who number thousands of thousands do the most needful labors for nothing, you poor freemen must starve for the want of employment. Do you, then, compel the Slaveholders to free us, and at the same time emancipate yourselves.

Then the freeman said: Never before have I seen that by holding you in bondage, I made myself a slave. Henceforth, I will struggle to free you, that your freedom may strengthen mine; for I fear, that if but *one* man be unlawfully held in servitude, the rights of all others will be in some manner injured.

II.

THE GREAT ROBBERY.

The Slave Power never keeps its Promises.

In a country in which the People had entered into a highly inconvenient partnership with Slaveholders for the enjoyment of national advantages, there arose a dispute between the parties for the control of certain territory which had been purchased with the money of the People. In this dispute, the Slaveholders demanded that a particular portion of this territory should be admitted to the common union with the full permission to themselves to hold certain of the People in bondage; but the People demanded that in this admitted district all persons should be free. In the National Council where this dispute was carried on, the controversy raged with great violence, and the Slaveholders menaced the deputies of the People with secession from the union unless their demands were conceded. Now to restore harmony between the parties and prevent the Slaveholders from ruining the People by secession, one of their order brought forward a plan of settlement. He proposed that a line be drawn through the territory, and that all on one side of the line, including the district about which the dispute arose, should be surrendered to the Slaveholders as a field for the display of the liberty they loved, and all on the other, should be guarantied to the opposing party for the development of their liberty. So the deputies of the People, alarmed at the threats of the Slaveholders, agreed to the proposed settlement, and they surrendered all the territory below the line, to be everlastingly desecrated and cursed, and the portion above, they reserved to the People and the uses of their freedom forever. This settlement they called a Compromise.

So the Compromise stood undisturbed for the lifetime of a generation—the Slaveholders proceeding forthwith to curse their allotted portion, and the People reserving theirs for the wants of their children. After thirty years and more had passed, there arose a Chief Magistrate who had been put in office by the Slave Power (for in their union with the People this Power managed to fill all the important offices of the common government with their own creatures), and this man longed for nothing so much as to signalize his servility to the class to which he owed his honors. He came, indeed, from that part of the country where the Slaveholder's liberty was limited, but contrary to what might be expected he cared little for the People, and worshipped their Masters. Fortunately for him, there was in the National Council a little man who had been raised to the dignity of a Slaveholder by marriage to a plantation; this order of nobility at times condescending to raise the common people to their own level by such a process.

This man having become a Slaveholder, professed a great regard for democracy, and thus had influence in the National Council. Sympathizing with the Chief Magistrate in his desire to subserve the interests of the Slaveholders, to whom they both owed their rise from obscurity, he hit upon the happy thought of robbing the People of their territory, and forthwith broached the matter to his fellow.

Said he to the Magistrate: We owe all we are, or ever shall be, to the Slaveholders. We are both small men—I, both in body and soul—you, at least, in soul. We need to do something to keep the remembrance of us alive after we have been cast aside by our party. If we cannot do a good thing, let us do a mean thing. Let us make the Slaveholders supreme over the People. Let us procure the passage of a law which shall surrender all the territory belonging to the People by the Compromise, to them.

Said the Magistrate: No one can have a more lively sense of his own littleness than I. By reading the papers devoted to our party, I can manage to keep up great impressions of my own importance; but in private, as soon as my mind is unenlivened by the incense of flattery, I sink back into a woful consciousness of my own insignificance. If my body, as well as soul, were small like yours, I should hardly know where to look for myself, when any great duty is to be done. But, thanks to heaven, nothing but my soul is *very* small. I agree with you that if we cannot do a great good thing, we would better imitate that Erostratus who burned the temple of Ephesus to be eternally remembered. I like the notion of robbing the People of their territory. But how shall we prevent their taking offense at it? When one cheats them he ought to contrive to conceal the act; for one often needs to use them after the deception, and that may be our case.

The People are asses, said the little man. Nothing is easier than to persuade them that the very act by which we cheat them of this territory is an act to extend Popular Sovereignty. Let us only spread among them that cry, and all who imbibe their democracy from their party leaders and from the magnetism of the national treasury, will at once accept it.

That is the true plan, said the Magistrate. Do you but draft a law for the government of that territory, in which there shall be just no Popular Sovereignty at all, and procure its passage, and my faithful editors will at once commence defending the fraud, and by unscrupulous lying the people can be made to swallow it without difficulty.

The plan was carried out; the law stealing the great territory was passed by the minions of the Slaveholders. But only a few of the People were sufficiently stupid to see in it the Popular Sovereignty which the lying editors so much applauded.

III.

THE STONES CRYING OUT.

That Nation which boasts most of its Liberty, is of all Nations most disgraced by its short-comings in securing it.

A NATION which had passed through a war of seven years' duration to secure liberty, and which had been led in the war by a great and good man, thought to honor him, long after his death, by building a monument to his memory. So they who directed the construction of it, recommended to the confederate States of the nation, that each should send a stone to the edifice, that when the work should be completed, there might be in its walls the enduring testimony that they had all shared in a common veneration of the great man, and in the glory of his monument. Then the confederate States sent in their memorial stones—one a piece of marble, and another a block of granite, and others such other stones as are seemly in an edifice, till all were represented. And the builders took the stones, and wrought them cunningly together, and the monument towered upward stately and fair.

Now it chanced, while the work was in progress, that the Chief Magistrate of the nation paid it a visit. And gazing on its beauty, he said: How majestic will this pile be when finished! For it will be a work which a king might desire for his mausoleum, but in which the very goddess of liberty can rejoice! Then the stones in the building, hearing his voice, cried out, all at once: Thou hypocrite! thou that executest a law returning slaves to bondage, and robbest unborn millions of freedom in the name of Popular Sovereignty, what is liberty to thee but the license of the strongest? Far rather would we now lie unpolished in our native quarries than to be brought together here to illustrate the disgrace of thy nation!—to hold up for the admiration of mankind the glory of her liberty, while three millions of slaves give the lie to her professions! For the groans of three millions of slaves force even us to cry out, when crimes that would blacken the darkness of hell a deeper dye, are sanctioned by the National Council, and executed by her highest officer! Speak not of liberty till liberty exists, or, at least, till we are scattered to the four winds of heaven; for how can we honor the Father of his country, when the country is not worthy of his fame?

Hearing these words the Magistrate hurried away, sensible of the reproof, but incapable of reformation; for though he had a glimmering apprehension of the demands of justice, he had a lively sense for the emoluments of office, and the pleasures of a perishable fame.

IV.

THE PEOPLE BECOME SOVEREIGN.

A community exercises Popular Sovereignty, when it is governed by Slaveholders against its will.

WHEN the people had been robbed of their territory by the annulment of the great Compromise, the cry of Popular Sovereignty echoed long and loudly among them, and many being desirous of erecting a state that should be truly free, flocked to the new country to create homes for themselves and establish liberty and justice. They said within themselves: Nowhere shall the people be more free and more happy, than under the institutions which we shall create. For all men without regard to race, or color, shall have their personal liberty guaranteed to them by immutable law, and naught but crime shall work a forfeiture of it. Ours shall be a community where the people are masters, and their will shall be law, because their aims will be just. A true brotherhood shall grow up in the virgin territory, which shall be an envied model to all other communities. The chains of no slave shall clank upon it, and no man shall eat the fruit of his brother's unpaid toil. There shall be equality before righteous laws, and no one shall serve another without his reward. Soon the wilderness shall bloom, and the solitary places be made glad for our coming, for we love the inalienable rights of man, and we go to prepare a garden wherein they may produce fruit.

Now the Slaveholders understanding better than the people what was meant by the sovereignty which they were to have, resolved to give them an example. For they did not believe in the equality of man with man, but in the ownership of man by man. When the people were ready to convene and ordain laws for freedom and justice, they therefore brought armed scoundrels into the new territory who assumed to themselves the right of legislating for the people, and appointing their rulers. These men enacted that inequality between man and his fellow should be the fundamental rule in the new community, and that the liberty of slaveholding should be first of all secured. And, therefore, they muzzled the mouths of the people, and tied their hands by accursed statutes, forbidding them to speak, or write, or vote against involuntary servitude.

Then the Chief Magistrate, beholding the result, said: The work is well done. The Slaveholders have their wish; they will henceforth be masters in the new territory, and this success of theirs will go far toward enthralling the People forever.

V.

THE CHIEF MAGISTRATE AND THE CHURCH DEPUTIES.

A part of the American Church is indifferent to the existence of Slavery, and a part devoted to it.

AFTER the People had suffered the Great Robbery of their territory in the name of Popular Sovereignty, and after the Chief Magistrate had appointed a governor to aid in establishing slavery in it, a Church in the South, being highly delighted with his proceedings, resolved to express to him their deep sense of his services. They therefore appointed deputies to congratulate him on the success of his beneficent projects, who went to his palace, and addressed him in these words:

We are representatives of a Church of Christ, which has witnessed your excellent official acts with the greatest interest. We are deeply imbued with the spirit of our divine Redeemer, and think we need to go to no one to be instructed in the principles of his religion. We sum up his whole law in two precepts; *Servants obey your masters*—and—*Let every soul be subject to the higher powers.* Having thoroughly studied Christ, we know that he came to redeem the world by subjecting man to man; and we suppose, therefore, that every institution which favors the control of man by man, must have a place in his especial regard. Inasmuch as your Excellency labors so zealously for the extension and perpetuity of the institution of Slavery, we feel that you are not only a model democrat, but a Christian on whom the divine blessing rests with a peculiar unction. The subjection of the People to the absolute authority of a few, if we study aright the Sacred Scriptures and the providential government of the world, seems to be the aim of the Universal Ruler. We look with no approbation on the prevalent clamor for liberty, nor indeed upon any scheme for the amelioration of human ills, which does not originate in the Church, and of which she is not patron. We regard the institution of Slavery as one of great beneficence, as sanctioned by Patriarchs and Apostles, and admirably adapted by its conservative and redemptive efficacy to the needs of the carnal man. We therefore strive with all diligence to subject the human mind to our dogmas, and then their bodies to an aristocracy with which we can sympathize. We feel that your Excellency is a co-laborer with us in this holy mission, and that you have done more in one year to perpetuate spiritual and corporeal servitude, than we could have done in ten by the application of our ordinary instrumentalities. Go on, then, noble Sir, in this mission of subjecting the People to their rightful masters, the Slaveholders, that a majestic aristocracy with which the Church can sympathize, may rule our land, and that she herself may be thus rendered glorious and terrible as an army with banners.

Then the Chief Magistrate responded: It was one of my first lessons in political philosophy that the People are not to be trusted with power. When, therefore, on attaining manhood, I found myself an actor in a political system in which the People were partners, I began to consider how I could most efficiently act against them. I soon discovered that the noble aristocracy of Slaveholders is the proper depository of the powers of our government, and its only competent managers. I also perceived that the People were so infatuated with the name and shadow of democracy, that they were utterly incapable of recognizing the genuine substance of it; and that there were parties in existence which were secretly striving to bring the People under the control of Slaveholders. But as certain crafty fellows who had succeeded in palming themselves upon the People as the exponents of genuine democracy, seemed most skillful in this business, I determined to become one of them, knowing that the name we bore would effectually conceal from the People any designs we might have against their liberties. Very fortunately for my fame, or at least, my notoriety, I have succeeded, in the name of Popular Sovereignty, in depriving the People of the rule of an immense territory, and in delivering it over to the Slaveholders. Unborn generations of this our American Nobility, I am sure, will regard me as their greatest benefactor. The skill with which I have stripped the People of possessions which they were unfit to manage, will never be forgotten.

But I am greatly rejoiced to hear through you the voice of the Church. For though the Northern Church while secretly sympathizing with you, maintains a wise silence, and dissuades from all agitation on the subject of Slavery, this open support of the Southern Church, commits her and the total body of the Lord's anointed to the defence of the institution. Thus in part openly supporting slavery, and in part conniving at it, the Church can be seen, as it were, in the very act of arraying herself in her beautiful garments; and though infidels may fancy they discover in them a resemblance to the color of the robes of the Scarlet Woman, we, who belong to the generation of the saints, know that this notion is altogether a mistake.

Aided by your prayers and sympathies, I shall go on in this noble cause; and I trust that during my Administration, Slavery will be so far nationalized, that the substantial power of the government will have passed finally and forever from the People, to the aristocracy of Slaveholders.

I beg you to receive my thanks for this open avowal of the real sentiments of the Church, and to be assured that while you shall receive the benefit of my prayers, the virtue of which is doubtless very great, you shall never see me faint in a cause like this.

VI.

THE COLONIZERS.

The main Obstacle to the Colonization of the African is his bondage.

CERTAIN good people of the free North, who were overflowing with benevolence, and in lack of any field of labor where it might find adequate vent, cast about for an object of charity. After diligent search their attention was drawn to the miseries of the African, and they resolved to pour out upon him all the milk of their humanity. And thinking that a man's natural home was the place where his ancestors were born, they went about the free North persuading the colored people that their home was the country whence their fathers were stolen. And while they persuaded the colored people to leave for this distant home, they cultivated the prejudices of the Anglo-Saxons, telling them that there was an ineradicable antipathy between the two races, which might one day dissolve in universal amalgamation. Others they influenced by representing barbarous Africa as a vast field for missionary enterprises, where the Cross might gain unheard-of victories. Thus by vigorous exertion of speech and pen, they built up a vast society to send African

Americans to a pleasant home among savages of their own race, who erect pyramids of human heads.

Now, when the society was fully formed, they convened in the city of the Capitol; and, before a large assembly, a colonizer stood up and spoke, saying: The process of removing natives of one country to their natural home in a foreign land, must necessarily be attended with some difficulties. The African labors under the illusion in all parts of our country, that he has a right to remain where he was born. Hardly can we persuade him that it is only the Anglo-Saxon who has a natural right to remain in the land of his nativity. It requires an immense outlay of Scriptural demonstration and profound discourses on the pedigree of the children of Ham, to bring him to a just sense of the rights and pretensions of our white race. But I would inform the audience, that by the aid of Scripture, and menaces, and invitations, we are making great impressions upon them. Granite does not wear away more rapidly under the continual dropping of oil, than the prejudices of the colored people against their natural home in a foreign land, vanishes under our preaching. No ocean was ever dipped dry with a thimble, sooner than we shall drain America of colored people by our scheme of colonizing. We may expect that in less than the combined lifetime of forty of the oldest of the ante-deluvian patriarchs, not a negro will be found this side of the Atlantic. Then look at the consequences upon Africa herself. Invaded by regiments of barbers, and boot-blacks, chimney-sweeps and kitchen-maids, cooks and hostlers, all soldiers of the Cross, how must the light of Christianity inundate that ill-fated land! The vision is too intoxicating to dream of! In Soudan a cook enters the service of some savage despot, serves up a dish of colored human flesh, tickles the palate of his majesty, exerts a moral influence, and before he is aware, the despot is humbled at the foot of the Cross! In Guinea, a colonized boot-black, taken captive a second time by a slave-dealer, puts an extra touch on his master's boot, drops in it a leaf from the American Tract Society, and forthwith the trader abandons his unholy occupation, returns with a few servants to America, and settles on a plantation in Alabama, an exemplary Christian! By such instrumentalities, and in such miraculous ways, is Africa to be redeemed. Not many geological epochs hence, and there will not be an unconverted heathen in that dark land,—not a colored man in America.

Then arose a Slaveholder and said: I am afraid I must mar the beautiful vision which the brother has just presented. He has spoken of the prejudice of the colored people against removal to Africa, as being an obstacle in the way of colonization. Let me tell him, that he will find us Slaveholders a greater obstacle than the prejudice of the negro. We know the value of the colored race in dollars and cents. Does he think we shall suffer them to be removed to Africa for any reason? Not at all. We have no horror of amalgamation, as half our plantations witness, and we care nothing of spreading the Gospel in Africa. We prefer rather that whole ship-loads should be brought here as slaves, and christianized by the discipline of the plantation. The natural road of the colored man to paradise, in our estimation, leads through the cotton-field and rice-swamp. Therefore colonization must stop, before it touches the slave. Colonize the free negro, if you will, but do not touch the bondman. This is the only legitimate province for the operations of your society. Thus you may be helpful to us. For we dislike the contagion of the presence of free negroes, among our slaves. Indeed, the first idea of colonization originated in our endeavors to remove this hateful class, and we think the movement should not extend to a class for which it was not originally intended.

In prosecuting the scheme of colonization, you may, therefore, if you choose, represent it in the North, as a plan to Christianize Africa, and to remove there *all* negroes: but in the South do not mention the idea of removing *all*, but only the *free* ones. The Slaveholder cares not a straw for your Society, except as it rids him of the embarrassment of the contamination of his slaves by the presence of freemen.

When this was heard, the assembly acquiesced, and ever after that the Society wore two faces;—one for the North, and the other for the South.

VII.

THE UNHAPPY FREEMAN.

The Southern Non-Slaveholder expects the Northern Freeman to do his Duty.

A NON-SLAVEHOLDER in the sunny South, sat, one summer's evening, in the door of his cabin, and gazed out upon the broad lands of a neighboring planter. As he gazed, he thought, with gloom, of his unhappy destiny, which, in a country abounding with thousands of acres of uncultivated ground, had allowed him none that he could call his own, and had ordained that he should never be a free owner of the soil. While indulging in these sad reflections, a traveller, riding along the solitary road that passed his cabin, halted and begged entertainment for the night. To this request the freeman answered, that if he could endure such poor fare as his cabin afforded, he was welcome to stay. So the traveller dismounted, and was soon sitting with his host engaged in friendly discourse, and watching the coming forth of the stars. But as the host's thoughts were not readily diverted from the subject which occupied him upon the arrival of his guest, he soon let fall expressions which revealed to the latter his mental disquietude; and upon the guest inquiring why he did not purchase a plantation and slaves, and become one of the lords of the land, the host answered:

You know little what it is to be a Non-slaveholder in the South. We have but one business among us by which a man can live. We are all tillers of the soil—Slaveholders and Non-slaveholders. But the Slaveholder, owning both land and slaves, forces the slaves to live at just so little expense to himself as will keep them in working order. He pays them nothing for their labor but *a scanty subsistence.* On the other hand, he gives the land a false value, by his slave system, which renders it impossible for the poor non-slaveholder ever to purchase any land but the merest patches; for the non-slaveholder's labor has no market and no market value, and large plantations are a necessity to the Slaveholder. The slaves are the greatest of curses to us. If they were all freed to-day, to-morrow we non-slaveholders might get a reasonable price for our labor. But now they all work for nothing, and we must work for nothing also. If they were free, they would set a price on their labor, and then we should be paid for ours. But, as matters are, if we were to live to the age of Methuselah, we never could purchase a plantation. We must rent, and fish, and hunt—or die. And I see not how we are to help ourselves. Though we are the majority, the greater part of us are so over-awed by the Slaveholders, and so dependent upon them in one form or another for the meager subsistence and slight employment we do find, that there is no courage among us to undertake extensive political combinations against the despots. I think, however, we should combine against them, if we saw any prospect that the free North would lead the way, and stand by us when we should attempt to emancipate ourselves. But how sad are our prospects, when we see northern freemen shouting democracy at the back of a northern President who opens entire territories to the control of the Slaveholder! We hope, and expect, some day to be redeemed; but it will never be till north ern freemen lay siege to Slavery from without. When that is done, we too will attack it from with in, and sweep it from existence.

Then said the guest: Take courage! In the North there are many who love liberty for the whole race. Not all there are hypocritical democrats. The North will soon do its duty, and you non-slaveholders of the South must be ready to strike when the hour comes!

Thus the host and the guest conversed together till the moon rode high in heaven, when they parted, each with more cheerful hopes of the final triumph of Freedom and Justice.

VIII.

THE CONGRESS OF REPUBLICS.

The Slaveholders wish to render Slavery more secure, when they extend the area of Freedom.

Two colonial States of America, subject to a great nation beyond the Atlantic, revolted from their mother country, and waging a vigorous war, attained their independence, and became free. But the mother country harrassed them, and keeping a depot of ships-of-war in the ports of an island near to their coasts, she constantly sent them on errands of mischief against the revolted colonies. These States therefore resolved to make a conquest of this Island, that there might be no harbor of refuge for predatory vessels near them. Now the Island was large and populous, disaffected, like the revolted States, to their common mother, and was crowded with slaves, which a part of the population held in the severest bondage. The rebel States sent delegates to a Congress on an isthmus joining the main portions of the American Continent, who were to devise plans to render their contemplated invasion successful, and to agree upon the terms on which their respective contributions to it were to be furnished.

Then the great North American, Anglo-Saxon, white and black, Slave-Republican Union, became very much concerned, and sent deputies also to the Congress. And the Secretary of the Union gave them a letter of instructions, which ran in the following words:

You are to represent to the new Republics, that our nation was once a colony which rebelled like themselves against the home government, and after a seven year's war attained its liberty, and became a power on earth. That, therefore, we cherish the deepest sympathy with all rebel peoples, and are ready, wherever we can do it with safety to ourselves, to extend the area of freedom, and loose the chains of the oppressed the world over. That the foreign policy of the Union has been distinguished by nothing so much as by the zeal with which she has scrutinized all corners of creation, in search of opportunities to smite the oppressor, and make herself respected as the champion of universal freedom. That she, therefore, feels a strong desire to aid the new Republics in establishing their independence on a secure foundation, and letting them share with herself in her own unequalled glory. But while she is anxious to render this assistance, she learns with great concern, that these Republics contemplate the invasion of the great Island near her coasts, and the emancipation of its slave population! Such an act, you may tell them, the model Republic does not approve; that she has very good reasons for not approving it; that she has three millions of slaves herself many of them contiguous to the coasts of the Island, who would at once arise in insurrection, and, on the plea that resistance to tyrants is obedience to God, would commit a wholesale slaughter of their masters; and that the contagion of the example of the emancipated hosts of the Island cannot be tolerated by the Proprietors of the model Republic. Tell them that these Proprietors, in extending the area of freedom, never forget their own cherished domestic institution, and that they are progressing rapidly in the domestication of the People with whom they are allied, in order to make the State more thoroughly a model for all rebel communities. By these statements you may perhaps suggest to them aspirations after a higher sort of liberty than that of which they have hitherto dreamed. But if they are insensible to the glories of such a liberty, tell them that we shall resist all invasions of that Island, which are to be connected with the emancipation of its slave population, with all the power of which we are masters.

When the deputies of the rebel States had heard these menaces from the Proprietors of the Great Republic, conscious that by an invasion of the Island they should be drawn into a war with her, as well as with the mother country, they abandoned the project of invasion, and to this day the greater part of the population of the Island is in bondage.

IX.

THE ORDER OF IGNORAMI.

One cannot be a Know-Nothing without being subservient to the Slave Power.

When the Slave Power in the Great Republic, by their aggressions on liberty, had aroused the People to a sense of their insecurity, and made them restive under their rule, they began to fear that they had carried their tyrannical attempts to too great a length; and they began to be anxious themselves, lest the People should become too conscious of their proceedings, and should, in a moment of great excitement, rise against them, and overthrow Slavery with a single stroke. Therefore, wise ones among them, foreseeing this possible result, counselled with one another how to avert it. And they said: The People are becoming awake to our plans and are beginning to understand our plots against their freedom. They are combining against us, the only genuine aristocracy, and a great party is growing up, which, unless we take measures in season to prevent it, will make Liberty national, as we would make Slavery. We have used the name and power of Democracy so long to cover our designs, that they are beginning to suspect that the word is a mere synonym for hypocrisy and deception. We must bestir ourselves and create a new party among them, to divert their attention from the great issue of Slavery or Freedom, and then when we have divided them among themselves, we will slip in, and legislate them all into Slavery, when they are least aware of it. Now there are a great many among them who have a very great and very foolish horror of aliens, and we will avail ourselves of this prejudice to create a secret society, which shall enlist among its members multitudes of their number, and arouse their hostility against these aliens, and turn their attention from us and our doings. We will call this society the Order of Ignorami. The name will be very attractive, for he who assumes it will secretly flatter himself that every one will recognize the bearer of the name as the possessor of some secret knowledge, which it would be very desirable to attain. But the name will really be an open secret to us, indicating that the poor fool who bears it is ignorantly a mere tool for us to use in our dirty work. There will be another advantage in the creation of such a society, beside setting the People at variance and diverting their attention from the issue of Slavery. The aliens who come to our country strengthen the People against us and our institution. They bring with them a love of a higher liberty than we can tolerate, whatever forms of despotism they may cherish; and they add overwhelming numbers to the ranks of the People. Hitherto we have blinded them to our proceedings by the cry of Democracy; but now that that is becoming somewhat stale, we must cultivate the prejudices against them of our narrow-minded natives.

In organizing this new party we must mix in the organization just a sufficient number of Slaveholders to manage it, and direct it to our purposes, in case political contingencies should make it powerful; and if ever it should nominate candidates for the two highest offices in the nation, we should take care that one of them be a Doughface and the other a Slaveholder.

Thus the Slaveholders counselled; and after mature deliberation the Order of Ignorami burst into light, a master-piece of Slaveholders' cunning, officered by men of their own class, and mustering in its ranks the most unleavened of the Doughfaces.

THE DANGEROUS WOMAN

X.

THE DANGEROUS WOMAN.

Even a Woman who teaches Slaves to read, is a terror to their Masters.

In one of the slave states of the Great Republic, a woman of gentle heart and humble aspirations, followed the avocation of a teacher. She had left her home among the green hills of the colder North to earn an honest livelihood in a sunnier land. Disposed to do good to all as opportunity offered, she was particularly delighted in aiding the truly needy, and in imparting instruction to such as were unable to instruct themselves. And in the country of her adoption she found abundant occasion for the manifestation of her benevolence, for she was surrounded by slaves to whom the law closed the avenues of knowledge. In her innocent simplicity she took compassion on many of these, gathered them together and instructed them in the mysteries of reading and writing. Her proceedings becoming known to the Slaveholders of the vicinity, their indignation was greatly roused, and they seized the defenseless woman and brought her to trial for the crime. And the evidence of witnesses being produced against her, and her own admissions, her guilt was clearly proved, and the judge proceeded to pronounce sentence in the following words:

Woman, you are charged with the great crime of teaching slaves to read and write, and from the evidence adduced the charge is most clearly proved, and it becomes my painful duty to pronounce upon you the sentence of the law. It is rarely that an offense of so grave a character is brought before this Court. Homicide, theft, and arson are crimes with which we are familiar, but the teaching ot slaves to read is a crime the rarity of which is equalled only by its enormity. The passions from which such a crime could proceed are almost unknown to the southern heart. The tree of knowledge does not grow on slave soil, and we are strangers to its fruit. We think but fair to presume that ignorance of the true genius and spirit of southern institutions, must have betrayed you into this crime, and as the Court wishes your amendment, rather than your ruin, we will state for your future profit the principles and grounds of these institutions.

They are free *par excellence.* They aim at the conservation of the choicest and most precious sort of liberty—that of *oppressing the weak.* This liberty is enjoyed by a select class of whites, who constitute the oppressors. The residue of the whites and all blacks, are the oppressed. As this species ot liberty can only be perpetuated by keeping knowledge from these two classes, the law, which in the South is made by the oppressing class, guards with great jealousy all the avenues of knowledge against the invasion of the slaves and the non-slaveholding whites. It is plain to see why this should be done. With the diffusion of knowledge would come inquiry into the justice of our social relations, and with this inquiry there would arise great dissatisfaction with their condition in the minds both of slaves and non-slaveholders. For first the slaves would begin to imagine that all men are created equal, that they have as just a right to life, liberty, and the pursuit of happiness as their masters, and that they are entitled to wages for their labor. But if our four millions of slaves were once possessed of these ideas, you yourself perceive that it would be very difficult for us to maintain our authority. The dissemination of such sentiments among them would create universal disturbance, and very dangerous excitement. Must we not, therefore, suppress them? Certainly. You see, therefore, no free presses, no free teaching, no free speech in the South; for these forms of freedom are incompatible with the liberty of oppressing others—which is southern liberty. But we exclude free presses and free speech from our borders not less to prevent excitement among our slaves, than among our non-slaveholding whites. For the slave institution not only muzzles the mouths of these whites, but degrades and impoverishes them. They feel the degradation and poverty, but they do not see the connection between these evils and the slavery; nor do we intend that they shall see them. And we therefore sedulously keep knowledge and freedom of speech from their reach, as from the slave. Even the Gospel we expurgate of all sentiments favorable to liberty, before we suffer it to be preached, and thus we think we have the institution invincibly fortified.

You understand, then, the reasons why we prohibit the teaching of slaves to read and write. We stand in great terror of the spread of knowledge. For the maintenance of our own liberties, and indeed of our own safety, absolutely demands a wide-spread and nearly universal ignorance.

It is not often, madam, that a judge in the South, sitting in open Court, ventures thus frankly to set forth the grounds and reasons of southern institutions. While we love our peculiar liberty, we feel a delicacy in openly avowing the policy we are obliged to pursue to maintain it. We would far rather dilate, on occasions like this, upon the manly grace and chivalrous features of the southern character. But when one is put on trial for the crime of teaching slaves to read, even though the person be a woman, southern courts are wont to forget all considerations of chivalry, and rush at once to the rescue; for even a woman is a terror to us when she teaches slaves to read!

The Court feels bound, madam, to visit upon you the utmost rigor of the law. You are sentenced to one year's imprisonment, where you are to be kept at hard labor.

When this sentence was heard, a murmur of general satisfaction pervaded the court-room. So the defenseless woman went to prison, and expiated her crime by a year's imprisonment.

XI.

THE HAPPY CANDIDATES.

Pleasant is the Union between Doughface and Slaveholder, when the People are to be cheated.

When the time came for the nomination of candidates for the Presidency, the Order of Ignorami selected, as had been before determined, a Doughface for President, and a Slaveholder for Vice-President. For as slaveholders were growing odious in the nation, the proprietors of the Order considered it politic to do the work of Slavery by putting forward a Doughface for the higher office. Being very suspicious of the free North, they naturally supposed the People to be suspicious of them;—fearing the People, they thought they were themselves distrusted.

Now accident brought the two candidates together after their nomination, and they improved the occasion to congratulate each other on their good fortune, and confer on the policy they should pursue, if elected.

Said the Doughface: After the signing of that Fugitive Slave Bill, I thought my prospects of nomination to the Presidency were very bad indeed. I had gone down as low in subserviency to your class as I could. Not that I would not have gone lower, if I had seen any advantage likely to arise from such action. But the People were becoming alarmed, and indignant at the existence of such a law, and I feared that even the Slave Power would not dare to put me forward as a candidate again. I notice that a public man must not do too *little* for your class, for then you distrust him; nor too *much*, for then you are fearful of his popularity in the North, and so reject him on the score of availability. You gentlemen of the South are a very exacting set to labor for. It requires a very nice combination of meanness, audacity, and cunning, to hold the first place in your favor, and thus stand fair for the Presidency. The present occupant of that office, it seems to me, possesses the first two qualities in perfection, but rather fails in the third. I flatter myself that, while the first two are no less *pronounced* in me, the third is in my composition more nearly on a par with the other two, than in him. I think I am a more natural candidate for the Presidency than he, in the present temper of the public mind. It is by my specific gravity, so to speak, in these three qualities, that I have risen like a soap-bubble, in the guise of an Ignoramus, to the very outermost surface of popularity. No puff-ball ever rode on an agitated horse-pond more triumphantly, than I shall bound over the waves of the political caldron during the present canvass. So much does a man owe to intrinsic worthlessness for his success as an Ignoramus. And after all, I am somewhat amazed to find myself a candidate for that high office. At times, I half suspect that I may have been of some advantage to the People, and that therefore I am nominated. But when I think of the Fugitive Slave Act, I know that my usefulness never secured me this great honor.

No, said the Slaveholder, it was not because you are any friend to the People that you are a candidate. The man that could sign the Fugitive Slave Bill, is *our* friend, not the People's. It was those three qualities of which you spoke, made so conspicuous and so illustrious by the signing of that Bill, which stamped you as ours. The man who, born in the North, can come forward voluntarily to aid us in humbling the People, and riveting still more closely the chains of our slaves, is the man whom we delight to honor. To honor, I say, that is, to give him office and money. You were nominated by us to be *used*. And if you are willing to be used, you shall have office and money while you live. As to your reputation, after you are dead, we Slaveholders cannot promise you much that is valuable. But possessing the three qualities of which you spoke, you probably care little about that. What do you propose to do if elected?

Of course, said the Doughface, I shall do all that in me lies to perpetuate the thrall of the Slave Power. I do not see how an Ignoramus can do any thing else. I should like to try my hand at a compromise, but the present incumbent of the presidential office has so nearly spoiled that business, that I think nothing more can be done at it. The establishing of Slavery in the free States, seems to me the only open field in which laurels are now to be won by a President. The extending of areas of Freedom southward may perhaps give me a little occupation. But if I were only President again, I am sure I could hit upon something quite as ingenious as the annulling of the old Compromise.

That you would find hard to excel, said the Slaveholder. But you need have no concern. We will find you plenty to do. Only be subservient, and consent to be *used,* and we will pay you in such kind of coin as you can appreciate.

As to myself, being the owner of a hundred slaves, though you may occupy the higher office, I shall naturally wish to lead, and be the real President. You would consent to that?

Of course, said the Doughface.

Then we shall have a very harmonious administration, said the Slaveholder. You occupying the Presidency, and I taking the precedency, all things will go on smoothly.

That it will, said the Doughface; and may we be elected!

There is little doubt of our success, said the Slaveholder. You know that I wear the skin of a dead lion.

I know it, said the Doughface. But can you not manage to stretch it so far over me, as to cover one of my ears?

Not well, answered the Slaveholder. By so doing I might expose one of my own; and you know the People do not need to see both ears of an animal to tell what it is. I will, however, lend it to you occasionally, if you will not attempt to roar. I wish to do all the roaring myself.

To this the Doughface consented, and after agreeing upon a time to make trial of the lion's skin, they parted in good spirits.

XII.

THE TRIAL OF THE LION'S SKIN.

The reputation of a Dead Hero cannot well be made to cover two candidates for office.

THE Order of Ignorami nominated a Doughface and a Slaveholder to fill the two highest offices in the land of the free. Now the Slaveholder owned the skin of a Lion, which he intended to wear during the canvass for these offices, in order to gain favor with the People. For when the Lion lived the People had made a great pet of him. But as the Doughface had no lion's skin, it was agreed between the candidates that they should wear it by turns. So they came together to try it on, and see how it could be made to fit both. And going into a private place apart from all spectators, the Doughface took the Slaveholder, and put his legs through the skin of the hinder legs of the Lion, and his arms through the skin of the fore legs, and enveloped his head in the bristling mane, and so completely concealed him that not a hair stuck out. But when the Slaveholder was arrayed in it, he began walk to and fro in the room, and his satisfaction was very great.

This, said he, seems to be a very good fit. I never felt so much like a lion before—I think I am

THE TRIAL OF THE LION'S SKIN

a lion. What will be the astonishment of the People when I come out in this dress? They will think it their old favorite Lion, or at least one of his whelps—won't they? Do my ears stick out? Look and see; for an exposure of those organs might ruin both our prospects.

Your ears are entirely hidden, said the Doughface. But would it not be well to get down upon all-fours? Lions do not walk about, you know, on two legs.

Of course I shall do so when I appear in public, said the Slaveholder. I was just walking about here in private on two legs, because it is natural, and then I wished to see myself. You need not tell me how lions go—I have seen lions. Does this mane look fierce?

Very fierce, said the Doughface.

Well; then I am satisfied, completely satisfied, said the Slaveholder. Ever since the old Lion died, I have had it in my mind to put it on, if I should ever be nominated to a great office. I would not venture before the People in my own natural skin for any consideration. It is only lately, however, that I have thought it could be used by both of us. Come, let me put it on you.

So saying he stripped it off himself and began fitting it to the Doughface. And he got the Doughface's arms and legs through the proper parts of the lion's skin without difficulty. But when he came to the head, he found it utterly impossible to confine the ears under it; for so often as one was closely shut in, the other flew out, and after repeated efforts to conceal them, the Slaveholder was obliged to abandon the undertaking in despair.

This is very discouraging, said the Doughface. I had no idea that my ears are so excessively large.

They are large, said the Slaveholder. I see no help for you except to cut them off. Then this tail hangs far to one side. Are you Doughfaces all so mis-shapen?

Mis-shapen or not, answered the other, we are as God made us.

As God made you! said the Slaveholder. You look more like the handiwork of the Evil One, Shall I clip your ears a bit?

If it must come to that, said the Doughface, I give up all hopes of using the lion's skin at all. In fact, I think I'll resign. I am greatly disheartened. The omens look bad for me, and if I run as a candidate, I can only play into another's hands. The Ignorami are disbanding, and under the circumstances, I think I must leave you to run alone. However, I will consider of the matter, and if there is any prospect of doing the People an injury, I will consent to continue a candidate; otherwise, not. You may take off the skin.

If you should resign, said the Slaveholder, I might possibly take your place as nominee, but at all events, I shall not surrender so long as Doughfaces can be found to work with me.

So saying, he took the lion's skin off his companion, and rolling it under his arm walked proudly away.

XIII.

THE CHRISTIAN SLAVE.

Good Christians sell better than any other class of Slaves in the South.

A SLAVE-DEALER visited a plantation to make an examination of the human cattle kept on it, to see if any would sell well in a more southern market. He lived by the profits of his sales; purchasing at low prices, and selling at greater, and made it, therefore, a rule to select the best samples for his distant market, for on these he made his greatest profits.

So the owner took him among the cabins, and brought out his slaves for examination. And the dealer looking over the lot was much pleased with one man of majestic figure, and round sleek limbs, the picture of physical health and strength. Looking at him for some time in silent admiration, the dealer finally inquired his name and price.

Then said the Slaveholder: On account of his manly appearance we call him George Washington, and on account of his meekness and docility, he cannot be sold for a sum less than two thousand dollars.

A great price to ask, said the dealer.

That is true, replied the Slaveholder. But he is a *Christian* slave. It is only yesterday that we partook of the sacrament together. And when I was partaking of the cup, casting my eye upon him, I thought it a great sin to part with him for less than two thousand. I have owned a great many slaves in my time, and have dealt with all sorts of characters in the capacity of a master. And let me assure you, that of all qualities in a slave, the Christian graces of humility and patience are the most desirable. He that can bear scourging, and branding, and partial starvation, which are essentials of the slave's condition, with Christian resignation, is the man for the plantation. We can get more labor, more cotton, more sugar, more money, out of such a one, than a half-dozen of the ordinary class. I love the Gospel for what it has done for my own soul; but shall I say, that I value it still more for its economic worth, in adding to the annual profits of our plantations? Give me the Christian slave, if I am to get the greatest possible crops at the least possible expense. They will bear lower feeding, and more scourging, without loss of strength, than any other class. And when this fact becomes generally known, we may anticipate a great triumph of the Gospel in the South.

I know, said the dealer, the value of Christian slaves, as well as you can. I make my best profits on them. If a slave prays and sings psalms, and is resigned to his lot, he will bring more money than one that does not. The piety enters as an element into his marketable value. And it seems to me that religion might well be encouraged on every plantation, if it can be done without putting the Bible into the very hands of the slave.

We can cultivate piety in them without any such hazardous expedients, said the Slaveholder. But what do you say to the boy? will you take him?

On the whole, said the dealer, as he is a Christian, that and his good appearance, and finally his name, determine me to the purchase.

So a sale was agreed upon, and the slave was delivered over to the dealer, to whom as he departed, the Slaveholder said: Let the boy partake of the sacrament occasionally, for that will keep him in good heart.

XIV.

THE STRONG ASS.

The North is a strong Ass bowing between two Burdens.

A COMPANY of Slaveholders being together at a convivial party, their conversation turned on the question whether the People could govern themselves. A part of the company strongly maintained that they could, because all the tendencies of human nature were toward Liberty and a true Universal Brotherhood, which the expansion of intelligence and natural benevolence must in time bring to pass. But the majority asserted that the instant large masses were combined in one political organization, there were developed powers of government which only the *few* could manage. The proposing of laws, for example, said one, must be done by a few, for multitudes cannot unite in suggesting the enacting of a specific law. Give me, said he, the initiation of laws, and I will manage to control any people. For it is an easy matter, during the lapse of generations, by proposing laws which apparently favor liberty, so to link one bad law with another, as to make their united action entirely subversive of it. To what do we Slaveholders owe our power to-day? Do we not govern this nation as we will? And why? Because our fathers made a compact with the representatives of the free states ostensibly to establish Justice and Liberty, but in the compact itself cunningly laid the foundation for an edifice of Slavery which should overshadow the whole land. For they forced into the compact this provision, that three Slaveholders should have as much power in the government as five Non-slaveholders. This was the germ of our present strength. Then the representatives of the free states allowed us to augment the number of our slaves for twenty years by importation, and bound the non-slaveholding People to deliver up to us our fugitives. As a pretended equivalent we agreed to pay direct taxes to support the government. What a compact! Our fathers said to the People, we will enter a Union with you if you will give us the control of yourselves; and in return we will bear a part of the expense of governing you! Was not that a magnificent offer? To be sure the People never thoroughly understood it. But the mischief of the matter is, they never can understand the bearing and ultimate issues of the laws their representatives enact. Witness the course of the national legislation for the last sixty years. Have not the People borne the heavy expenses of two wars entered into, and carried through, mainly to perpetuate our power? Have we not added to the Territory of the Union by war and purchase an area nearly equal to that of the original colonies, in order that we might manufacture slave states? Do the People to this day, however, know what we have been doing? Not at all. We have divided them among themselves, and created parties among them, all of which fear each other's political success more than ours. Of course we govern the People through them and their devilish demagogues.

Nothing exhibits the stupidity of the People in a stronger light, than their blind adhesion to the *name* of democracy. Our successes are achieved under that name, laughable as it may seem. For we have got the name, with all the power devotion to it ensures, to mean nothing more than fidelity to Slavery. And so strong is the infatuation of the North for the shadow without the substance, that if we were to propose a law that every white man in the country, destitute of a hundred dollars worth of property, should be sold as "a bondman forever" to the highest bidder, and offer it as a democratic measure, it would be received with a shout by their non-slaveholding voters. Miserable wretches that they are! Prating of democracy and equal rights, yet ready to run in crowds to lick up the dust at our feet! Stupid dolts! who pour out their blood and treasure for us in war, who add constantly to the area of Slavery, and chase negro slaves with alacrity, who can expect that their eyes will ever be opened? They neither see nor feel whither they are drifting; or if they see, they are too obstinately devoted to their party-leaders to do otherwise than they are bid. However, loaded down as they are, they have as much as they can bear, and the device on their banner should be a strong ass bowing between two burdens.

And what should the burdens be? said another of the company. What, indeed, replied the first speaker but that Slavery with which we load them, and the Democracy which their doughfaces saddle on them?

XV.

THE SLAVEHOLDER ENSLAVED.

It is right for a Slave to run away from his Master.

A Slaveholder possessed a docile and obedient bondman, whom he made steward of his household, and whom he held in such high confidence as to entrust him at times with the keys of his strong box. The slave lived in plenty, and needed nothing to his physical well-being and comfort. But he still longed for his freedom, for he aspired to higher things than bodily ease and enjoyment. And he often petitioned his master for this great and priceless boon. But as often as he asked it the master took advantage of his ignorance and his sense of religious duty, to prove to him, out of Scripture, his obligation to be a slave. And the master would also endeavor to persuade him that freedom was not a natural right, but a privilege conceded to a few by the laws of civil society. Unable to answer his master's arguments, the slave submitted to his condition as to the command of God, thinking it indeed to be the Divine will.

Now it chanced that the master resolved on a journey in foreign lands; and, that he might pass the time more pleasantly, and cast the burdens of travel on another, he took with him his faithful bondman, and went to sea. They had not been

"They ran away together." Par. XV.

many days on their voyage before they were captured by pirates, and carried captives to a hot and sickly land, where both master and slave were sold into slavery together, and both fell to the same purchaser. Tasks of intolerable severity were laid upon them, and for slight offenses terrible scourgings were inflicted upon both by the same lash. These sufferings gendered in the mind of the master more profound meditations on Slavery than had ever before entered his mind, and produced inward comments on Scripture that were entirely heterodox in his native country. Thus, as he sat one evening supping on crusts of stale bread, moistened with filthy water, he requested of his former bondman to beg of their new lord freedom for both.

That I do, said the slave. But though our lord is a Mohammedan, he is well versed in Moses and the Christian Scriptures, and whenever I broach the subject, he says to me: Servants, obey your masters—and cites the case of Onesimus, and tells me that so long as I continue a Christian he shall hold me a slave, but if I choose to confess Mohammedanism he would be bound by his religion to set me free. I am not inclined to acknowledge the Prophet, and you long since proved to me that Christianity recognises and sustains Slavery.

So I thought, said the master, till I tasted Slavery for myself. But now I recollect that Jesus enjoined upon his followers first of all to *love one another, and then all mankind as brethren.* Even Paul recommended the master of Onesimus to receive him back as *a brother beloved.* Now when one man treats another as a brother beloved, he cannot allow that brother to be considered as *property*. And though Paul said: Servants obey your masters—I appeal from Paul drowsy, to Paul awake, ordering the master to receive Onesimus as a brother beloved. Tell him this, if he will argue the matter with you. But if he will not hear to reason, let us escape from his power.

But is it right, said the bondman, for a slave to run away from his master?

It is not only right, said the master, *for a slave to run away from his master, but it is wrong for any one to oppose his escape.* Now that I am a slave myself, I perceive this to be a self-evident truth, which no argument can make clearer, and nothing but sophisms can obscure.

Hearing this reasoning the bondman's scruples were removed, and, watching their opportunity, master and slave *ran away together;* and, coming to the sea-coast, a ship picked them up and brought them to their own land.

And now the emancipated Slaveholder, taught a lesson by experience, freed all whom he held in bondage, and paid back-wages to as many as would receive them. For, said he, all men have a title to the possession of their own bodies, and the workman is worthy of his hire. But the bondman with whom he himself had suffered Slavery never left him, for now Onesimus had, indeed, been received back as a brother. And when the Slaveholder died, he remembered his great act of justice, and passed away in quiet joy.

XVI.

THE LYING SLAVE.

If Slaves are Liars, their Masters make them so.

A STRANGER journeyed from the North and took up a temporary residence in the family of a Slaveholder. Here he devoted himself to the instruction of his host's children, and having an inclination to the careful study of whatever came under his observation, he gave particular attention to the manners and habits of the slaves, as well as the subjects of his teaching. For he had learned to consider nothing which concerned the welfare of man as disconnected from his own. Among the facts which he observed was this, that when the slaves received their weekly allowance of provisions, a scanty supply was too often doled out to them. And this was so frequently repeated, that he became certain that the slaves must make up the deficiency by their own wits, and at the master's expense. It chanced that walking late in the evening over the wooded portion of the plantation upon which he resided, he came upon two of them who were in the act of dressing one of the fattest of the master's porkers. Approaching within ear-shot, he learned from their conversation that they had stolen the animal, and that they were devising how to conceal the theft. He quietly withdrew, and determined to note the result if a discovery of the theft should occur.

Not long after this he was surprised to see the thieves and a dozen others, drawn up before the master to be questioned about the missing animal. And as the question went round, as to each one's knowledge of its whereabouts, all stoutly maintained their ignorance. But the master, certain that some among them had stolen it, took all and scourged them severely; for he thought it better always when many slaves stand under a common suspicion of guilt, to punish the innocent with the guilty, rather than suffer the guilty to escape.

A few days after the scourging, the stranger privately informing the two slaves that he had knowledge of their theft, inquired why they had not manfully confessed it.

Then one of them answered: We act always from fear. Through fear alone does our master keep us in subjection. And knowing that this fear is the only motive through which he can compel us to do his will, he constantly distrusts our sincerity in his service. But this distrust in him continually begets in us that of which he suspects us—*deception.* We constantly endeavor to shirk the labor he puts upon us, while we pretend to be diligent, because we have no motive to work for him but fear. Thus incessantly acting a lie, how can we do otherwise than speak lies, when we think our occasions demand them. When you, O stranger, shall act for your fellow-man only from fear and coercion, then will you know what it is to be, indeed, mean, base, and miserable—and an habitual liar. We are liars because we are slaves; and we shall continue to be liars so long as we are thus degraded. But the master who makes the slave, makes the liar. Set us free, and we shall learn to love the truth, act it, and speak it. For as Slavery genders falsehood, so does Freedom beget truthfulness.

Then replied the stranger: Sad is your fate, indeed. It is new to me that Slavery makes men liars. But it is so; and the last man to complain of the lies of a slave, should be his master.

XVII.

FREE TRADE.

Slaveholders desire to cripple the Growth of the People.

In a country where Slaveholders rule the People, the latter, favored by an excellent climate, and a noble domain which abounded in minerals, and was traversed by noble rivers, established the manufacture of cloths and iron, and cultivated such arts as were needful to their happiness. Magazines of innumerable commodities, and enormous engines lending strength to the arms of industry, abounded in the home of the People. Labor was honorable, and Poverty, with his lean and sallow face, began to be unknown among them.

The Slaveholders, amazed at their growth, endeavored to wring from the sinews of their bondmen, resources as great, and an equally varied abundance. But the skill was wanting, because the bondmen had no motive for exertion, and in lieu of the cultivation of all arts, and the production of every variety of commodities, their industry took one channel, and was engrossed by a single avocation. They tilled the soil, and did nothing beside, while the overseer's lash was the cause of all their wealth.

Mortified at their own weakness, and constantly irritated by the sight of the People's prosperity, they tried violent expedients to prevent their growth. They first shut up the ships of the People in their own ports for a long period, hoping that when commerce was prostrated, their great strength would decline. They next plunged them into a three years' war. But, as in process of time, the People recovered from this misfortune, they began to devise expedients to accomplish the destruction of their prosperity, in a way which should be slower, but more sure.

And they said among themselves:

We shall never be able to keep the People in subjection, nor effectually cripple their strength, so long as they are allowed to maintain such a diversified industry. For, the multiplication of avocations furnishes so many incentives to exertion, and so increases opportunities for hireling labor to dictate its own terms, that the masses will escape from our control in spite of all we can do. There is but one way to keep them down. *We must abridge the number of their avocations, and branches of industry.* If we reduce the greater part of them to the tilling of the soil, and as many as possible of the residue to be mere carriers and transport agents, we shall achieve our object. For if the mass of the People become agriculturalists like ourselves, as our laborers *work for nothing, and their support costs next to nothing*, we can easily subject the free agriculturalists to our power, by underselling them, and thus diminish their number as freemen, by converting them into a *tenantry*, which, for our purposes, is almost as favorable for us as if they were slaves. For free homesteads are the strength of the People; and if we make it impossible for any but large land-holders to live comfortably by agriculture, *the masses will cease to be freeholders.* And we must abridge the number of branches of industry for this simple reason: as in civilized life every freeman is obliged to produce *more* of one kind of commodities, and *less* of all others, than he needs, the greater we can make the majority of laborers producing one kind of commodity over those producing all others, the less valuable will be each man's labor engaged in producing that commodity. Thus, if we force the mass of society into one avocation, the poorer we shall make them, and the more dependent on master-capitalists. We have, then, but to limit the number of avocations among which the choice of employment is to be made, and the more will that branch of industry which requires the least skill—agriculture—be over-crowded, and a general state of dependence among those engaged in it, like that on our plantations, prevail.

Our policy, then, should be to persuade the People to buy, where they can do so most cheaply, at money prices. To this end, we must induce them to purchase all the necessaries of life, except food and fuel, at the farthest possible distance from home. This will extinguish most of the arts and manufactures which require skill, and over-crowd agriculture and the transit avocations. By this policy we can, in time, make the greater part of the

People a tenantry, tilling no land of their own, or hirelings without family or home, and then they will be, in fact, slaves.

Thus the Slaveholders planned, and thus they persuaded the People to act—who, thenceforward, like a blind Samson shorn of his strength, staggered on toward poverty and despotism.

XVIII.

THE DANGEROUS MAN.

In half the Union it is unsafe for a Freeman to avow Sentiments hostile to Slavery.

A Non-slaveholder, in the Great Republic, journeyed into the far South, to spend the winter, and ply the trade of a carpenter. Skilful in his calling, he readily found employment, and gained much favor with the villagers among whom he resided, both for his skill's sake and because of his companionable qualities. But the villagers, being great devotees of democracy, were naturally zealous for the perpetuity and extension of Slavery, and watched with suspicion the conduct of such as came among them from that section of the Republic where the blessings of that divine institution were unknown. And certain of them inquiring of the northern freeman whether he believed it lawful for one man to hold another in bondage, and whether the citizens of a free state were not morally bound to capture and return to the master his fugitive slave, he promptly answered that man could not rightfully hold property in man, neither could a freeman return a fugitive to bondage, if he regarded the higher law. When it was noised abroad in the village that the carpenter held such sentiments, the rumor caused a great commotion, and the prudent citizens called a public meeting to take into consideration the proper means of defense against a peril so great as the presence among them of dangerous sentiments. And when the meeting was convened, a democratic Slaveholder arose and spoke as follows:

Fellow Citizens: If I were to inform you that a barrel of gun-powder is now beneath the building in which we are assembled, and that a slow-match already kindled is in contact with it, your horror would be beyond expression, and you would either rush headlong from the house, or leap at once to extinguish the match. Fellow citizens, a greater peril is upon us. Lend me your ears while I carefully describe it. It is well known that a northern mechanic has been amongst us for some time, apparently pursuing his calling without a thought of our domestic institutions. So industrious and steady has he been, as to gain the confidence of many of our citizens. But a few of us, suspecting that the latitude in which he was born was not so favorable to the growth of rational political ideas and pure democracy as the sunny South, resolved to sound him as to his opinions touching human bondage We found that he had been secretly thinking of our domestic institutions; and we even made him avow that he considered Slavery immoral, and that he held the recent Fugitive Slave Law not to be binding on a freeman's conscience! These opinions are in the highest degree dangerous to us, and our system of society cannot tolerate the presence of men who entertain them.

No one, fellow citizens, believes more sincerely than myself in freedom of thought and freedom of speech, but I believe also that both should be restricted by a delicate regard to the demands of the institution of Slavery. There should be just so much freedom of thought and speech tolerated, as a chivalric and manly devotion to sound democracy, and the bondage of the greatest number, will allow. But northern men should be carefully watched; for, as a general thing, they think and speak too freely, though I except from this charge the so-called northern democracy, which, so far as I have observed, never thinks at all, and always acts for us and Slavery.

I would recommend, fellow citizens, that this man, caught, as it were, in the very act of entertaining dangerous sentiments, be warned, forthwith, to leave the town within twenty-four hours, under penalty of a coat of tar and feathers.

This speech was received with a murmur of general approbation, and it was resolved that the secretary of the meeting be instructed to notify the mechanic of the resolution, and warn him in a kindly way of his danger.

The Secretary, therefore, wrote him in these words:

Sir: It has come to the ears of the citizens of this place, that you entertain dangerous sentiments, and even go so far as to avow them openly. A meeting has just been holden in which your case has been considered. It was proved before all present, that you believe human bondage to be immoral, and the Fugitive Slave Law of no binding obligation! These sentiments the meeting recognized to be in the highest degree dangerous, and the person holding them they voted, unanimously, unworthy of a residence in this community. We know that by the Constitution, freedom of speech and thought is extended to citizens of any one State resident temporarily in another, but we do not understand that provision of the Constitution to allow a northern freeman to think and speak against Slavery south of Mason and Dixon's line. The great privileges guaranteed to the North by that instrument are, to support the national government, provide offices for Slaveholders, pay southern postage, extend the areas of freedom southward, and nurse a democracy to cherish and perpetuate Slavery. But as you, in violation of these constitutional guarantees, have foolishly assumed to entertain and avow sentiments hostile to Slavery, it is ordered by the meeting, that you leave town within twenty-four hours, under penalty of a coat of tar and feathers.

The meeting allow me to inform you, however, that if on returning to your native State, you shall commune with your fellow citizens who are national democrats, imbibe their spirit with all its issues, and by a becoming servility acquire an honorable standing in their ranks, your past dangerous sentiments shall be forgotten, and you shall be allowed once more to take up your residence among us, and be admitted to full fellowship with the proprietors of the Constitution, and the true lords of the land.

When the mechanic had received this gentle monition, he quietly packed his tools, and journeyed to the north of Mason and Dixon's line, knowing that the Constitution of his country could not guaranty freedom of thought and speech in the South.

XIX.

THE APOSTLE OF LIBERTY.

Lying for Slavery is so well done by native Americans, that Irish Apostles find it an unprofitable business.

THERE arose in Ireland a leader of the people, who, thinking them to be grievously oppressed by England, endeavored by speech and pen to arouse them to a sense of their servile condition. To this end, he vehemently proclaimed the praises of liberty, and presented such glowing pictures of the happiness and glory of free nations, that he kindled among them an ardent desire for independence. For he showed that all men are, by nature, free and equal, and that no man has a right to govern another against his consent, neither one nation another; that man as man has the natural right to the control of his person, and every nation, the right to self-government. And he often held up the example of America to encourage his people to separate from England.

So stirring were his appeals, and so violent his denunciations, that the people began to prepare for forcible resistance. But the constituted authorities, becoming alarmed at his proceedings, and at his influence over the ignorant, seized him and put him on trial for sedition and treason. And the evidence being strong against him, he was condemned, and sent as an exile into a savage country far from his native land. But faithful to his principles, and loving freedom too well to remain a prisoner, he improved the opportunity which fortune offered him and made his escape, for he thought himself justified in fleeing from unjust confinement. And after his escape he came to America, the land of the free.

Now in America, more than in any other country, is the genuineness of a man's love of liberty severely tried. For Slaveholders own a sixth of all the People as property, and govern a large proportion of the residue in the name of Democracy, so that very few of the white natives dare to consider even their souls their own. Into this crucible of the love of liberty the Irish Apostle plunged, and the fires being hot around him, he soon proved to be dross. For now being in a country where small men lead the People under the patronage of Slaveholders, a certain latent servility and love of popularity, which had lain dormant while he was in Ireland, rose to the surface of his character, and became ruling passions. And he became a lying editor, and began to play sycophant to the Slaveholders. And he recanted his faith in the rights of man, and advocated only the rights of Slaveholders and Irishmen, so that he might become a popular leader. But his journal did not flourish, because his readers cared little for Irishmen, and the emigrant Irish cared little for him, and the Slaveholders had more native lying editors than they needed. And he fell into great fits of despondency, and wished himself back in Ireland, raising rebellion again. In one of these fits, a Slaveholder accosted him, and asked how he prospered.

The Apostle of Liberty answered: I fare badly. In Ireland I led the people, and did all in my power to stir them up against England. For I wished to be a popular man if I could be. And knowing no better way to do this than by making them dissatisfied with their condition, I sat about praising liberty and denouncing oppression. And at that time I did really love liberty, and spoke with some zeal and sincerity, and my appeals were heard by the people, and I should have brought them to open rebellion, had not the government seized and sent me abroad as an exile. But I escaped and came hither, hoping that my reputation as a martyr to liberty would secure me a fat office and a great deal of glory. But I have in some manner lost both the office and the glory. And now I long for nothing so much as a plantation in Alabama, and a hundred negroes. But how shall I get them?

Then answered the Slaveholder: Your case is hard, and all the harder that your merits are considerable. You took up a very unprofitable occupation when you came here. The business of a lying editor, especially if he is a defender of our domestic institutions, is one that certainly deserves the approbation of all good men, but it does not pay well just now, on account of the number of natives engaged in it. Nearly all of our journals which advocate Slavery are conducted by such editors. An alien, however great his hypocrisy, and his capacity to lie, cannot compete with a native when defending Slavery. After praising liberty in Ireland, you did right to apologize for Slavery here, but you can make nothing at it as a business, as the ill success of your journal shows you. All that is necessary to be done in the way of direct lying the editors perform, and as to the mystifying the popular mind, that is done by our ministers of the Gospel. Your desire for a plantation in Alabama is very commendable, and highly becoming in an apostle of liberty. But these plantations cost money, and we cannot afford to bestow them gratis on such persons as often as they arrive from foreign lands, for at that rate we should be soon forced to take up the occupation of apostles ourselves, being absolutely driven from our homes by the invasion of armies of friends.

As circumstances are, I would recommend to you to seek a secluded nook somewhere in the country, and wait till the demand for lying editors, or some other class of liars-for-slavery, has risen to call forth your talents, and supply you with bread. Wait patiently, and in time, if you are not popular, you may at least continue notorious.

So the Apostle abandoned his journal, and set to waiting for an opportunity to become famous. But the longer he waited, the less conspicuous he became, till he sunk at last silently and quietly into utter oblivion. For even his transient notoriety was forgotten

XX.

THE SLAVE-PEN.

There should ever be a Slave-pen within sight of the Capitol, to remind Aliens of the quality of American Liberty.

A NOBLE Exile who had suffered much and worthily at home in behalf of humanity, came to America, to witness the reality of that liberty, the hope of which had been to him like the cloud by day and the pillar of fire by night. For the fame of America's freedom had traveled far among the nations, and multitudes had been soothed in their oppressions by the remembrance of it. To see the most illustrious example of devotion to America's liberty, he sought the presence of her Chief Magistrate, who entertained him with glowing pictures of her institutions, and her political and commercial prosperity. Now the Magistrate, wishing to leave upon his guest the most favorable impressions, took him through the streets of the city of the Capitol, and showed him with great pride the beautiful edifices which the free government used. With all these the stranger was greatly delighted, and began to think that freedom had indeed found an asylum on earth. While gazing in quiet pleasure on these tokens of prosperity, and these first essays of a free government, he inquired the use of an edifice much less imposing than the rest, over which the national flag was flying, and which bore even a filthy and *slattern* look.

That, said the Magistrate, is a slave-market. You may not be aware that our government is a union of Slaveholders and the People, and that by the compact of union, the former have more power in the government than the People themselves, and that simply because they are Slaveholders. This, however, is true. In America, the liberty of slave-holding is the most precious sort of liberty, and democracy itself with us, means, the *government of the People by the slave-holding minority.* Hence, when the Masters of the People come up here to legislate for them, they wish some refreshing symbol of their power to be ever within sight. And, therefore, this slave-pen is established near the Capitol, in order that the Masters and youthful Democrats, who come hither as law-givers, may draw a living inspiration from the scourgings within its walls. And when the Slaveholders have subdued the People, and established their own democracy, we intend to blend the device of an overseer's whip among the stars of the national flag. The stripes are on it already, you perceive, and they have a beautiful significance. Look, therefore, O stranger, on that slave-pen as a symbol of our American freedom.

Then the Exile exclaimed: Much have I suffered by the treachery of pretended friends, and the open assaults of bitter enemies; and much have I endured to aid the down-trodden millions of the old world, struggling for a freedom that never comes; and ever the faith that one great nation at least is free, has sustained my flagging strength, and nerved me against a total despair. But now my heart dies within me, when I find that true freedom has no refuge on earth; and that the so called land of liberty is but a country where a People full of hypocrisy licks the feet of tyrants and forges fetters for their slaves. O give me back the open oppression of the despots of the Old World, and let me never see again the monstrous liberty of the despots of the new!

XXI.

THE WEIGHING OF THE MERITS.

Our Presidents are the Tools of the Slave Power.

Two ex-presidents meeting together began to compare their deserts, and when one insisted on a good thing he had done, the other set against it a similar good thing. But as neither could claim superiority, they determined to write on separate billiard balls the distinguishing acts of their administrations, and then to cast them into the opposite scales of a balance, when he should be considered to have been the most worthy magistrate who had cast the heavier ball. Then one wrote:

I secured the enactment of a law returning every fugitive bondman to his master. And the other wrote: *I robbed the People of a vast territory sacred to liberty, and made them believe that the act of robbery secured the establishment of their own sovereignty.*

Then casting the balls into the scales, the arms swayed to and fro for a moment, and finally settled in equilibrium. But as they were wondering at the exact adjustment of the balance, a Slaveholder looking in at the door cried: Flunkeys! there is no difference between you; your deserts are equal. Not what you did for the People, constitutes your merit, but what you did for us. We are willing to take the will for the deed, where nothing better can be had from a president. But your services for Slavery are really very great. For one of you converted all the free states into a slave-pen, and the other nipped all future free states in the bud. The subjugation of the People to our control must date emphatically from the era when you two were successively in office, and it is impossible to tell which was most thoroughly devoted to us. You deserve nothing from the People but curses, therefore, from us expect your reward. We cannot make you presidents again, for you have rendered yourselves suspected by the People. But we will give you a flunkey's wages, something that will satisfy your appetite for public places, and while it renders you unpopular marks you as ours. For though we use traitors to subdue the People, we never forget to mark them with that brand.

Then said one ex-president to the other: To this have we come! We have cheated the People only to be despised by those who have used us.

But the other said: I care not for the People, nor for honor from them. They have their masters. Those masters I serve, and I would rather be their flunkey, than to occupy any other place. It suits my genius and taste, for nature made me to crawl, rather than soar. I shall never regret deceiving the People, so long as I am well paid. Besides, the People wish to be deceived; let them be so.

XXII.

THE DEMOCRAT ON A HUNT.

The latest Democracy finds a genial occupation in the Chase of Fugitive Slaves.

A NORTHERN DEMOCRAT visited that section of the Union where Slavery prevails. And desiring to become thoroughly acquainted with his southern brethren, he made himself at home among them. He traveled from plantation to plantation on noble steeds provided for him by his entertainers. But they feasted and flattered, and flattered and feasted their guest till his head was turned by "the hospitalities of the South."

Meanwhile these hospitable people were secretly measuring the strength of his anti-slavery convictions, and some of them resolved to put them to a practical trial. So they gathered together from many quarters with horses, and hounds, and guns, prepared for a hunt, to which the Democrat was invited. When they were ready to set out, the guest asked his companions what kind of game they expected to take. To this his friends laughingly replied, that they should keep that a secret, in order that he might experience an agreeable surprise.

The hunt began, and away they went with whoop and halloo, through open field and forest, till they were finally brought to a stand by the baying of the hounds in a thick, and almost impervious swamp. Here the hunters dismounted, and our Democrat with the rest pushed forward, as best he could, till the *game* was discovered, defending itself from the hounds, bloody and faint from a desperate fight.

Here, said the Slaveholders, is our game—and their guest, looking, was for a moment startled to see a Fugitive Slave keeping the dogs at bay. But recovering at once his natural democratic composure and servility, he said: There is no action more becoming a good democrat than this. Democracy is exhibited in one's obeying the powers that be, whatever they may ordain. I regard your order, noble Slaveholders, as the proprietors of the constitution, the proper depository of all national authority, and the power to which the People, particularly Non-Slaveholders, owe allegiance. And I may say, that though, if I had an uncultivated conscience, I might feel some repugnance to a work like this, I have notwithstanding been so thoroughly disciplined in the theory and practice of human rights by our National Democracy as to see clearly that the maintenance of the rights of Slaveholders is the primary object of our government; and that only by the perpetuation of the institution of Slavery, can our country become the home of liberty, and a refuge for the oppressed of all nations. It was for liberty tinctured with Slavery, I may add, that our fathers bled and died.

Then the Slaveholders praised their friend for his patriotism, and for the possession of a conscience so cultivated as to see human rights in their proper relations; and particularly did they extol that lucid clearness of vision which enabled him to discern the primary object of our government. So on their return from the hunt, they placed him at the head of their company, where he displayed his love of liberty, and the purity of his democracy, by inflicting many an unfeeling blow on the recaptured fugitive. By these manifestations of servility the Slaveholders, behind his back, were greatly delighted, and one said to another: If we can but keep alive this temper of mingled cowardice and cruelty in the breasts of the Northern Democracy, our reign over both Slaves and People will be eternal.

XXIII.

THE BLACK EMBASSADORS.

The Ministers of Colored Nations cannot be received by the Government of the Union.

A NATION of Blacks, who were once Slaves, wrought out their freedom through much suffering and bloodshed. Wishing now to be numbered in the great fraternity of nations, they established a republic, and sent abroad ministers asking to be recognized as an independent people. Among the despots, and constitutional kings of the world, these ministers were every where received kindly, and the independence of their people recognized.

Other ministers were likewise sent to a sister republic, not many hundred miles from their own island, to demand recognition. But here their suit was denied. For thc rcpublic to which the colored embassadors came, was based on a union of the People with Slaveholders. And the Slaveholders held Blacks in bondage, and by the terms of the compact of union, they were to have greater power in the government of the republic than the People themselves, simply because they were Slaveholders. And they not only managed to control the government, but to diffuse a most violent prejudice against the Blacks among the People, and a great fear of the black color as such.

When, therefore, these colored embassadors arrived, the slaveholding proprietors of the government met to devise means to thwart their errand. And in secret conclave some spoke as follows:

It will be a dangerous precedent to suffer these Blacks to be received in the capacity of embassadors of a foreign state. For if they come thus, the contrast between their condition as freemen, and our own slave blacks will be so strong as to awaken among the representatives of the People a feeling that there is something wrong in Slavery, and it will make the Slaves themselves restive and discontented, to see men of their own color elevated to such stations. Besides, if we thus openly recognise the justice of the independence and freedom of this colored nation, we shall as openly condemn ourselves for holding their brethren in bondage. And while we are publicly greeting black embassadors as representatives of a free republic, our hypocrisy will not only be painful to ourselves, but what is worse, apparent to all the world. For it is not a bad thing for us to be hypocrites, when we derive great advantages from such conduct, but it would be exceedingly disagreeable to have our hypocrisy revealed. Now the People do not as yet even suspect us to be hypocrites. But a public recognition that a black republic may rightfully exist, would open our real character to the knowledge of all. We must therefore contrive to prevent the recognition of these Black Embassadors, and at the same time, conceal the reason why we prevent it.

So it was secretly resolved among them to adopt this policy. When therefore the representatives of the People met in the national council, a Slaveholder rose and spoke at great length on the odiousness of the black color; showing among other things that blacks were descended from Ham, and that the curse of Canaan rested on them; and that the sole reason of their being admitted to America was, that by the inscrutable wisdom of Providence they might be made missionaries to Africa; and that moreover if colored embassadors were admitted and the independence of their nation recognized, Amalgamation would be spread far and wide, and would soon debase the color of the universal Anglo-Saxon race. By these and similar arguments, he so wrought on the delicate sensibilities of the timid representatives, that they rejected the ministers as they would have done so many public lepers, and congratulated themselves at the same time, that they had saved the nation from a great disgrace. But they did not perceive that they had brought on themselves a greater, by refusing to recognize a people's independence which had been acquired by great sufferings and losses, thus treading under foot the rights of man.

XXIV.

THE OPENING OF THE SEALS.

When the People bargain with Slaveholders they ever get cheated.

Two European monarchs, learning that the People of the colonies which had recently revolted from England, and become independent, were about to establish a compact of union with Slaveholders, disputed as to which of the two parties would be the loser, one monarch contending that it would be the People, the other, that the Slaveholders would lose. But admitting that some length of time must elapse before the dispute could be decided, they agreed to state the point in question in writing, and seal it up, and that after sixty years it should be opened by their descendants for their instruction, and the advantages gained either by the People or their partners, should be concisely stated, and the document again sealed, not to be opened till after the lapse of another sixty years. So when the time prescribed had passed, and the monarchs had gone the way of all mortals, their descendants opened the writing, and in accordance with the agreement made this statement:

We find that in the articles of compact between the Slaveholders and the People, it is stated that the Union is formed to establish Justice and Liberty. But we find in the articles themselves, the People guaranteeing the secure possession of their slaves to their masters. We find them agreeing that three Slaveholders shall have as much power as five Non-Slaveholders. We find the Slaveholders agreeing to be taxed directly for the support of the Union, in return for those stipulations on the part of the People. We therefore find the People losers in the compact itself.

As to the performance of the stipulations, we find the People faithfully performing their agreements, returning fugitive slaves, and consenting that five of their own number should equal but three Slaveholders, forming their national Congress by that ratio. On the other hand we find the Slaveholders paying no direct taxes for the support of the government during sixty years.

As to the administration of the government, we find that the greater part of its civil officers, its embassadors, the commanders of its Army and Navy, in short most of its power, has been in the hands of Slaveholders.

As to the history of the government, so far as it has acted for either party to the disadvantage of the other, we find that after the national Treasury had been pretty well filled by the People, many millions of their money were extended to buy a large territory for the Slaveholders from the French.

9

We next find the Slaveholders shutting up the shipping of the People in their harbors, in order to prostrate their commerce, and keep down their power.

But as the People were not sufficiently crippled by that act, we find the Slaveholders, under pretences of maintaining free trade and sailor's rights, forceing them into a war with the most powerful of nations, which again cost hundreds of millions of the People's money.

The People still continuing to prosper, we find the Slaveholders persuading them in the name of Democracy, to destroy most of their manufactories of Cloth and Iron, and send their Gold and Silver to foreign countries to buy them.

Notwithstanding these drawbacks, as the People, continued to increase in numbers and wealth, we find the Slaveholders, in fear that the free states would outnumber their own, sending marauders upon the territory of another nation, to seize and annex it to the Union as a slave state.

We next find the Slaveholders making war upon this same nation, at the cost, to the People, of a hundred millions, and again robbing its territory and annexing it for themselves.

Still fearing the People, we find them next, by bribery and menace, persuading the deputies of the People to deliver over to them all the unoccupied territory of the Union to be made into slave states, so that the government might be forever in their hands.

Thus far, then we find the People losers, and we know not that it shall ever be otherwise. But we set down this statement as to the workings of the compact, that at the end of another sixty years, those who come after us may see who are then the gaining party.

Then the document was again sealed, to be opened once more at the appointed time. But no man knows who then shall rule in the Great Republic.

XXV.

THE REJECTED OFFER.

A Fugitive Slave knows when he is happy as well as a born Democrat

A SLAVE who had escaped from bondage, found a home in one corner of the Union, where liberty was respected, though not secure. Possessed of nothing but his hands and a healthy body when his life of freedom began, he yet managed to accumulate, within a few years, much money, as well as houses and lands. He had not only gathered property, but he had learned to use it generously for the good of others, and thus the increase of his wealth did not make him feel poor. For his property did not possess him, but he possessed his property.

It chanced that this self-emancipated bondman, taking a journey, fell in with a man who had been a democrat from birth, as he said, and who pretended to know a great deal about liberty and the rights of man. Now the Fugitive, willing to try the value of his companion's regard for liberty, inquired of him whether a slave might lawfully run away from his master.

Then the Democrat said: Right and wrong depend upon relations. One set of relations makes an act right, a different set, makes it wrong. Of course the power which establishes the relations, makes all there is of right and wrong. In society, the Law ordained by the supreme power, determines the relations, and so determines the right and the wrong. I am inclined to think there is nothing higher than the Law, to make the difference between these things. What the law ordains, that is right; what it forbids is wrong. Where the Law permits Slavery, it is right; where it is prohibited, it is wrong. Now in our country the Law allows Slavery, that is, it gives permission to one man to own another. Therefore, the owner has a right to possess him whom the Law has put in his power. Then, of course, he who is owned cannot lawfully run away.

Then said the Fugitive: If you should take me by force, and carry me into a country where your bare claim to own me should make me your property, would your title to my person be just?

Certainly, said the Democrat. For justice in that country would allow me to own you.

And if, said the Fugitive, I should run away from you, would it be the duty of whoever could do it, to return me to my master?

It would, said the Democrat; for every good citizen should obey the law, whatever it commands, for that is to do right.

Then said the Fugitive: I have been a slave, and I ran away from my former master; and what is more, I intend to stay away.

Then the Democrat, surprised and confounded,

began to upbraid him for violating his duty and the Law, but finding that his reproaches did not move the Fugitive, he opened in another strain.

Said he: I see not why a slave in our country should run away. He is in a far better condition as a slave than a freeman. He has no cares and no anxieties. His master provides for him,—he is well clad, well sheltered, and well fed. What more can a reasonable man ask? Food, clothing, shelter, freedom from anxiety,—these are the great natural wants. Whoever has these supplied should ask for nothing more, for these are the main objects about which the struggle of life goes on. All these things you had as a slave. Here you can get nothing more, nor so much. A southern slave's situation is really better than to be poor and needy in the North. I would advise you to return, keep the Law, do right, obey your master,—for this is your true happiness. You cannot be happy as a freeman.

Then said the Fugitive: Since the case of a slave is so much better than that of a freeman, let us compromise our differences. My place as a slave is vacant. I know what it was,—how rich in food, clothing, and shelter — how free from care—how jolly. I also know what it is to be a freeman, and have a freeman's cares, and a freeman's struggles for a livelihood. Let us change places. I will continue here, and be a democrat in your place, shouldering a freeman's responsibilities. Do you go into the South, to my old master, lay aside your democracy, or at least so much of it as is not bred in the bone, and get the food, clothing, and shelter, for nothing. The exchange of situations will be vastly to the satisfaction and prosperity of both of us, I doubt not.

Then the other, taken entirely unawares by the novelty of the proposal, answered—he knew not what—but, blushing, stammered forth these words: It is just as well to be a northern Democrat.

You are right, said the Fugitive. The northern Democrat of to-day *is* a slave.

XXVI.

THE RULER OF A FREE PEOPLE TRIED.

The Chief Magistrate of a Free People needs not necessarily be a Man.

A SLAVE in Virginia ran away from his master, and coming to the Potomac he swam over it opposite the city of the Capitol. And seeing before him a large white mansion, he thought he would boldly approach the door and ask for refreshment and refuge from his master, who he knew would soon be in pursuit of him. So knocking at the door, it was opened by a lackey, to whom he told his story, and asked for admission. But the lackey hesitated when he knew that it was a fugitive slave who stood before him, and kept plying him with questions, while he meditated what to do. But a personage who had seen the slave approach, and had overheard the object of his visit, put his head out of an upper window, and asked him what he wanted.

Then the slave, looking up, said: I am a fugitive from one who calls himself my master. I am weary and hungry, and having swam the river, I wish to rest here a while and dry my garments, and get a little to eat. For it is a long way to Canada, and

"I am not a Man, but a President." Par. XXVI.

I must rest where I can, and depend on charity for food, for I have no money, and I expect that my master will soon be in pursuit of me.

Then the personage looking down from the upper window, said: This is the last place in the world for a fugitive slave to find refuge. This is the President's House, and I am the President of the American Union,—and a democratic President, too, and my chief business is to catch just such fellows as you.

And the slave, looking up, said: That cannot be, for I see on yonder Capitol the flag of liberty, glittering with stars, and the eagle, with wide spread wings, holds in his talons the arrows fatal to tyrants. Surely every man within the shadow of the Capitol must be worthy of carrying such a banner.

How simple you are, said the President. That flag only signifies that this land is the home of the oppressed of all nations except its own. We use it when we march against fugitive slaves. It is the same one that floated over the soldiers of the army of the Union, when they were called out to recapture Anthony Burns.

Who was Anthony Burns? said the fugitive.

Anthony was a run-away like yourself, said the President. He not only ran away from his master, but from his Church. He got away as far as Boston, and there one of my officials trapped him, and as the fanatics of that city tried to rescue him, I ordered out a good part of the army and navy to hold him; and, by a great outlay of national treasure, he was held, and returned to the lash of his master, and, by the blessing of God, to the very Church from whose Gospel he had tried to escape. So you need not try to do the same thing. I could send out, in less than an hour, the military force of half the Union, and the prayers of multitudes of clergymen, for your recapture. I am the great guardian of our domestic institutions. The Union is a great institution for catching fugitives, and my function is to marshal all the hounds, the two-legged and four-legged, in the chase.

Then leaning forward from the window, and rubbing both hands in sight of the slave, he continued: You need not come here for refuge. I am the man who executes the Fugitive Law, of which I know you have heard. And I do it with alacrity. It is natural to me. I like it. I have something of the bloodhound in my own composition — and something of the turkey-buzzard. Do not come to me for displays of humanity. I am not a man, but a President — a democratic President. So, away with you, or I will myself take you back to your master.

The Slave answered: If I had known that this was the house of the President, I would not have asked for charity here. But I thought it was the house of a man. So turning on his heel he fled hastily away, and the President shut the window, and the lackey the door, each in great disgust.

XXVII.

THE SLAVEHOLDER'S PROTECTION.

A body of ignorant Non-Slaveholding Freemen support the Tyranny of the Slaveholders, and degrade themselves.

Two Slaveholders, returning to their homes on an evening following an election, the younger of the two said to the elder:

It is a matter of surprise to me to see so many Non-Slaveholders voting with us. They have no interest in maintaining our aristocratic privileges, but on the contrary are acting in direct opposition to their own welfare. Strange as it is, they are zealous supporters of our institution, not only by their votes, but in other ways. They shout and halloo for Slavery as if the salvation of themselves and their children depended on its everlasting continuance. A word in reproach of it is sure to arouse their fiercest anger, and they are as ready to fight to maintain our supremacy over themselves and our slaves, as we are. They whose interests are all on the side of emancipation, are the most sturdy and blind in their hostility to it. The rude violence that suppresses free speech among us, and jeopardises the life of any assailant of our power, is mostly their work. I confess I do not understand this state of things; and as you have had more experience of life than myself, I should be pleased to have you enlighten me on the subject.

I perceive, said his friend, that you are not fully initiated in the mystery of the working of our free institutions. It requires the utmost care and attention to manage our social and political system to prevent its entire derangement, and as you are just about to become an active participant in it, you may, perhaps, be benefited by some suggestions gleaned from my experience.

You observe that the greater part of our Non-Slaveholders are extremely ignorant. Even the rudiments of knowledge, the simple arts of reading and writing, are not understood to any extent among them. Out of this ignorance grow certain vices, which flourish all the better the more dense the ignorance. I refer particularly to drunkenness, to the pride which is ashamed of labor, to the recklessness of human life, to that revengeful and contentious temper which is never satisfied with peace and good order. Now this class of our population, with all its vices, is absolutely indispensable to us. And, therefore, we nurse it with the greatest care.

We systematically cultivate their ignorance, with its attendant vices; and this is the first element of political knowledge to be acquired by a slaveholding statesman.

I can give you an example how we manage. It is well known that the northern Free States foster and cherish what they call a *common school* system.

This is well enough where the whole population are equal before the law. For if you wish equal rights in a community, they must be sufficiently educated to know what social and political arrangements will guaranty equal rights. But in a community where a slaveholding class is to rule, the less knowledge in those below that class, the better. For, where Slavery exists, the community is naturally divided into three ranks,—the Slaveholders, the Slaves, and the Non-Slaveholders. It is plain, that if the two latter classes know their rights, they will combine and overthrow the power of the Slaveholders. For that power is not only an injury to the slave, but to the freeman who lives beside the slave. It is an injury, because the freeman's labor is worth nothing where unpaid labor competes against it.

Then in the South we should guard against the spread of *common schools;* which, indeed, we do. For, though we pretend to take a great interest in the matter, it is nothing but a pretence. We can establish colleges and high schools, because the *kind* of education acquired in such seminaries being expensive, lies beyond the reach of our Non-Slaveholders, and even when acquired *leaves a prejudice against social equality* in the mind of the recipient, being mostly classical and scholastic, and everywhere tinctured with reverence for the slaveholding worthies of Greece and Rome. So you find that we cherish colleges and select schools, to the prejudice of *common schools,* where the People 'earn, and thus our Non-Slaveholders spontaneously grow up in ignorance of their rights and of the oppression which our system secretly works upon them. Along with this ignorance, grows contempt and hatred for the slave, and a desire to see him kept in servitude, so that where this passion has taken root, it becomes a defense and bulwark of our slave-system. For this hatred of the slave, makes our Non-Slaveholders a volunteer police force to keep them in bondage. The fools are our body-guard, our unpaid Swiss, in the South, out of blind antipathy to the slave forging his fetters and their own, with strokes of the same hammer.

But this folly and ignorance in them, you perceive, is all to our advantage. Their very vices are the materials of our prosperity.

There is another aspect in which the utility of the Non-Slaveholder's ignorance can be seen. Our slave-system requires a great deal of land for its effectual maintenance. It is thus crowding our Non-Slaveholders off all the good soil of the country. At present, they run away into our western territories, occupy the lands, and prepare the way for us to follow with our slaves. Then in time we come after them, settle down and make slave states where they have been pioneers. And thus we keep adding new slave states continually, to the Union. After a little time, we shall have so much impoverished all our Non-Slaveholders, North and South, and shall have occupied so much territory, that there will be no classes left but Slaveholders and Slaves throughout the Union. This glorious result will be brought about by cultivating the ignorance of the People. It is already so dense, that they do not see what is our object in adding new slave states to the Union. Their descendants may, perhaps, understand it, but it will be when they are no longer free.

The simple reason, then, why the Non-Slaveholders among us vote as we wish, is that they are profoundly ignorant of what they are about, not knowing that the same chain which passes around the neck of the slave is fastened to their own heels; and also, because they hate the slave too much to do him justice. But this hatred, again, springs from ignorance. They know that Slavery causes their own poverty, but they do not see that *our power* causes the Slavery.

By all means, then, cultivate the ignorance of the People, if you would secure your privileges as a Slaveholder; there is no other secure foundation for them.

When the young lord had received this explanation, he was very much gratified, and thanked his companion as he parted from him, for he thought by following the advice given him, he might one day become a legislator, deserving a seat in Congress.

XXVIII.

THE CRACKED LIBERTY-BELL.

The cracked Bell which announced the signing of the Declaration of Independence, is the symbol of our National Freedom.

A SLAVEHOLDER and a Doughface visited the hall of the Declaration of Independence in Philadelphia. And as they walked to and fro in it, in pleasant converse on the sacrifices of the revolutionary fathers, and their exertions in behalf of liberty, they pointed out to each other the places in the hall which they imagined the signers of the Declaration to occupy when that instrument was adopted. Here was the seat of the noble Hancock; there were the seats of Adams and Jefferson, and here sat Franklin. Among the things which attracted their attention, was the bell that had been rung as a signal of the adoption of the Declaration. Approaching it they examined the inscription: Proclaim Liberty to all the land, to all the inhabitants thereof.

Then the Slaveholder, examining it, said:

Those words are rather fanatical. Liberty should not be proclaimed to all the land, to all the inhabitants thereof. That would disorganize society. The greater part of men should serve their betters. A few should rule, and even own the masses as property. That is the way we do in the South. We have outgrown not only the sentiment inscribed on the bell, but the Declaration ot Independence also. We do not believe that all men are born free and equal, nor with equal natural rights to life, liberty, and the pursuit of happiness. That extravagant doctrine did good service at the time it was proclaimed, for even we Slaveholders then were in danger of being politically subjected to the oppression of the mother country, and we needed to arouse the yeomanry of the land, so that by their aid we might maintain our liberties. And it was a good stroke of policy, then, to arouse extravagant expectations of liberty in every one. But it was never intended to make a practical application of the principle. And so Slavery, domestic and political, exists in the South to this day. By the former kind of Slavery, we own men as property; by the latter, we disfranchise and govern a large part of our non-slaveholding freemen. Both the sentiments on the bell, and that of the Declaration, are fanatical and disorganizing. They proclaim too great a liberty, and the bell is cracked because the doctrine is false.

Then said the Doughface: I acquiesce most heartily in the sentiments you have just expressed.

But as they were about to leave the hall, having satisfied themselves with the contemplation of the memorials contained in it, a voice proceeded from the bell, and, to their astonishment, uttered these words:

You say rightly that the inscription on my face proclaims too great a liberty. He who inscribed it designed me to utter the glad tidings of freedom without regard to race or sex. And he sent me, a hundred years ago, when my voice was yet clear, from a country where a king, lords, and a dead Church, weigh down the freedom of the people, to this land, expecting that I should have naught but gladness to dispense, whenever my voice should be heard. Once, and once only, did I speak with joy, and proclaim liberty to all. But my joy has departed, and my voice has been restrained. For the Lord, seeing that I should speak ever after to a nation of hypocrites, inflicted upon me this hideous crack, that whenever I did speak, there should issue from me nothing but a miserable clatter, that should be in keeping with a Slaveholder's praises of liberty, and the peans of Doughfaces. Nor shall I ever speak again in clear and ringing tones, till Liberty *has been* proclaimed to *all* the land, to *all* the inhabitants thereof.

Upon hearing this, the listeners hastened in great alarm from the hall, the Doughface clinging to the arm of his friend, for they thought that a spirit had spoken.

XXIX.

THE RIGHT VICTIM.

The Fugitive Law enforced on a Democrat makes a Man of him.

A CITIZEN of the free states, who always shouted long and loudly for whatever the leaders of his party pronounced democratic, was particularly gratified with the enactment of a law restoring fugitive slaves to their masters; and whenever he came into the presence of Slaveholders he took occasion to speak very flatteringly of the statute. And what he said, that he practised. If a fugitive passed through his neighborhood he was ever ready and willing to join in the pursuit. As a professed democrat, he was wont to refer to his zeal for the execution of the Fugitive Law as proof that his democracy was genuine.

Living near the line that separates the slave and free states, he was as often in the one territory as the other, but ever the same advocate and defender of whatever the Slave Power made law. It happened that certain Slaveholders who had often heard him defend their institution, and had witnessed his activity in their cause, grew sick of his servility and meanness, and determined to give him a taste of the sweets of Slavery. So, finding him on his own territory, they kidnapped him, and were about to hurry him away into Slavery. And this they would have done at once, if certain strangers had not interfered in his behalf. But even their intervention availed little. For, his kidnappers bringing him before one authorized to decide the freedom of fugitives, the facts of his case were inquired into, and false witnesses were produced, who swore that they had known him a slave, and knew him to be the property of his captors. The democrat protested that he was a freeman, and a free citizen. But the dark complexion which nature chanced to have given him, and curly hair, with the false oaths, and the bribe of ten dollars which the law itself offered the judge who should condemn any one whose liberty was in question, all wrought against him, and he was pronounced a slave,—even the strangers who had interfered to save him, abandoning his cause. So he was taken away to a distant part of the country, and sold at auction for a high price.

He had hardly gone into the possession of his master before he commenced the story of his wrongs, telling how he had been kidnapped and brought before a United States Commissioner, and had lost his liberty by the oaths of false witnesses, and that he was a democrat, and had ever been one, and had helped execute the Fugitive Law himself.

When the master had heard all this, he immediately took him to the nearest tree, and, stripping him to his bare back, tied him up by the thumbs and ordered his overseer to give him forty lashes. So the overseer plied the scourge, and at every blow the skin flew in ribbons, and the blood streamed down, while his merciless master stood by, reviling.

Impudent scoundrel, said he, talk to me of your being a freeman! I am used to such tricks. Every run-away is a freeman till he is caught. But you think to escape by calling yourself a democrat likewise. A pretty device! I know not where you have learned the word. But I am the only democrat here, and I will give you a sense of its meaning. Lay on the lash, overseer! Teach him the rudiments of democracy!

So the free citizen groaned in bondage for months, and every time that he opened his mouth to talk of his freedom, he received his inevitable forty lashes. But, at last, becoming desperate, he put every thing at hazard, and, fleeing, safely reached his former home.

But never thereafter did he utter a word in favor of the Fugitive Law, nor did he justify Slavery, nor huzza for Democracy.

XXX.

THE POLITIC SLAVEHOLDERS.

The dread of Disunion, and the cry of Democracy are the means with which the Slave Power subdues the People.

A COMPANY of Slaveholders assembled to devise ways and means to perpetuate the Institution, and to rally about it the strength of the whole nation, that they might be forever the People's masters.

Then one among them arose and spoke as follows: The pillar of all social order is to have, in a community, as few free-holders as possible. For the more freeholders there exist among a people, the more equality there is among them, and of course the more independence, and the less disposition on the part of the many to submit to the rule of a few.

With us in the South, the authority of the few over the many is on a permanent basis, because we have a large slave population which we govern as we choose, and own as property. And the presence of these slaves among our non-slaveholding freemen makes the labor of the freemen cheap; so cheap that it is impossible for many of them to be freeholders. So that we govern them with our slaves by the same bond and lash. For by the control of the slaves we get control of the land, and make our non-slaveholding freemen first homeless and landless, and at last servile.

If we wish, then, to make our authority as Slaveholders permanent in the nation, we must make Slavery national. We cannot, however, do this at one leap. We must first subject the territories to the rule of Slavery, and creep on by degrees until we get it legalized in all the free states.

In those states, we shall have two classes to deal with. The one consists of the men of small properties, who follow the lead of the wealthy capitalists; the other is made up of the landless poor. The first class we must intimidate with threats of disunion, for to their leaders disunion means *loss of southern trade*, and they will act as their leaders order. These leaders' interests are in harmony with ours, and after a time they will begin to understand, and act with us cheerfully. For the wealthy traders of the North who make their fortunes out of the labor of others by profits, and who return no equivalent to society, are in principle nothing less than Slaveholders. But at present we must subdue them by fear of disunion.

With the landless poor, and so many of the small freeholders as we can influence, whose interests are entirely adverse to ours, we must pursue a different policy. While the virgin territory of the Republic is settling, we must encourage the monopoly of the soil by large landholders, and as Slaveholders can take up and occupy more territory in the same time than Non-Slaveholders, we must establish the principle that Slaveholders have equal rights with them to the territories of the Republic. For when we establish the principle of our *equal* right to the land, we can easily take possession of the *greater* part of it, and absolutely control the legislation.

Now as the landless poor, and small freeholders, are always taken with names, and never desert their party-leaders, we must compel these leaders to raise the cry of Popular Sovereignty and Equal Rights, to delude their followers. For as thieves elude pursuit by shouting, Stop thief! so we, by raising a prodigious din about Popular Sovereignty, Democracy, Constitutional Obligations and Rights, can gain all our most cherished ends under the pretense of supporting, what we aim with all our might to destroy.

Then another said: I approve of the policy suggested. A persistent threat of disunion will keep the wealthy classes of the free states subservient to our purposes; and by shouting *Democracy*, now that the word has become a mere party-badge, we can deceive the northern rabble, and lead them whither we will. I am much mistaken, if in a few generations, we shall not have brought them to the level of our slaves.

So the meeting dispersed, and a loud cry for Democracy forthwith filled the air, and from that hour the name became national, but the substance vanished.

XXXI.

THE TRAITOR TO THE UNION.

Hostility to Slavery is Treason to the Union.

One of the People, plainly clad and of unprepossessing appearance, was passing the palace of the Chief Magistrate of a nation wont to boast of its freedom. It occurred to him to propose a question to that great officer. So knocking at the door, a lackey bowed him in, and gave him a seat in a sumptuous apartment. Then as the plain man sat and viewed the furniture and ornaments about him, he said to himself: Surely splendor like this is designed to grace only the abode of Liberty's favorite servant. The whisper which is abroad among the People, that this great functionary is really Slavery's high constable, cannot be true.

As he thus meditated, the Magistrate came forth, and with a bland voice, and democratic smile, asked his pleasure. Then the plain man said: I have a question to propose to your Excellency. State it, said the Magistrate. Said the plain man: If a hundred Slaveholders should hold a Convention to prepare for a dissolution of the Union, and a hundred of the people should convene to devise measures to resist the return of Fugitive Slaves, which would be the greater criminals?

The Magistrate answered: Clearly the hundred Non-Slaveholders. For though the Constitution declares that the Union was formed to establish Liberty and Justice, we who administer the government hold that purpose to be only the ostensible object of that instrument, which can be proved in this way: The primary object of government is the protection of Property: If that be duly protected, the owners of it will take care of Life and Liberty. Now property in man is the most valuable species of property; and as the Constitution gives to Slaveholders privileges in legislation superior to those of the People, simply because they are a higher class of beings, liberty, in the constitutional sense, must mean the privilege of slaveholding, with extraordinary guaranties, which is the noblest, choicest, and most desirable kind of liberty. When, therefore, Slaveholders conspire to secede from the Union, there is properly no spirit of treason in the act, for they in a manner stand above the Constitution, as the nursing and rearing of Slaveholders is its great purpose. It exists only to procure them advantages and delights. On the other hand, the obligations and burdens attendant on the working of that instrument are expected to fall upon the people—the Non-Slaveholders—and they stand under the Constitution. When, therefore, the latter convene to resist the laws for the return of Fugitive Bondmen, such an act is in the highest degree insolent and treasonable, as showing disrespect to their masters, and as tending to restrict the liberty of slaveholding, thus being, moreover, anti-democratic. In bare dislike of Slavery there lies latent treason, and enmity to Democracy. We avoid even this latent treason, we keep near the other extreme. We love Slavery *and* Democracy. So in the discharge of our official duties, we sometimes call out the Army and Navy to aid in restoring Fugitives; while on the other hand, if Slaveholders should actually take up arms against the Union, or against a nation with which we are at peace, or should attempt to usurp the government of a non-slaveholding state, we should be so far from opposing such action on their part, that we should openly support it.

Here the plain man grew restless, and rising hastily, bowed low, and went quietly and swiftly from the door, while the Magistrate gazed after him with his democratic smile.

XXXII.

THE INGENIOUS JUDGE.

It is only in a Republic that the Writ of Habeas Corpus can be used to recover Fugitive Slaves.

A Slaveholder, taking a journey, was pleased to traverse a free state, and for the convenience of his family, took with him a female servant. For it is the fashion of his class to do no menial service for themselves which they can thrust upon another. On the journey, the master and servant passed through a great city, where many dwelt who held the rights of man in greater reverence than those of masters. They supposed that as no man could justly make slaves of them, no one could justly do the same by others, and having learned that men should not do unto others that which they would not that others should do to themselves, they endeavored to make this precept a rule of life.

Several of these friends of humanity, hearing of the transit of the Slaveholder, came hastily together, and, meeting him as he was about to leave their city, one of them told the slave openly, in her master's presence, that she was free. Upon this, he who announced her freedom went quietly away, while others, gathering around the slave, took her under their protection.

But the master, grieved and vexed at the loss of his property, at once set about the recovery of it. And going to a Judge of the nation, he demanded that he who had told his slave of her right to freedom, might be brought by some writ to show cause why he detained the Slaveholder's property. This Judge, willing to gain the favor of Slaveholders throughout the country, considered with himself what he should do.

I know of no better way, said he, to recover this slave than to issue the Writ of Habeas Corpus. It was originally designed, it is true, to deliver those unjustly in bonds, and it will be a novel procedure to refasten with it bonds justly broken. But if liberty can be overthrown in the name of the People's Sovereignty, why cannot the Habeas Corpus be converted into a trap to catch slaves? I should hate to fall behind the Chief Magistrate in cunning devices to favor the institution. I, too, wish to achieve a reputation among Slaveholders. Long after I am gone, will they remember the Judge who caught a slave in so ingenious a way. If it should ever be said that such a use of the Writ is unlawful, employing it to recover property, I can reply that it was used by me to recover a *person*. I will, therefore, issue it.

So he issued the Writ, commanding the friend of the slave to show cause why he unlawfully detained the person of the slave woman. But the slave's friend answered that she had never been in his keeping, thereby affirming the very truth.

Then was the Judge angry because the Habeas Corpus had failed to catch the slave, and said: Am I not the keeper of my brother, the Slaveholder, and the keeper of his rights? As his slave has escaped through the connivance of this man, his vengeance, at least, shall be gratified. I will therefore assume that her champion lied in responding to the Writ, and I will keep him in prison on a charge of contempt of court, till, through the force of suffering, I compel him to acknowledge the lie which I have falsely charged upon him.

So the Judge sent the friend of the slave to prison, where he lay in long and harsh durance, suffering by virtue of the newly vamped Writ of Habeas Corpus, which at the same time exhibited the Judge's base ingenuity, and the disgrace of his nation.

XXXIII.

THE PROTECTION OF LAW.

Citizens of a Free State barely suspected of aiding the escape of Fugitive Slaves may be sent to Prison in a Slave State.

A CITIZEN of a slave state in the Great Republic, became deeply interested in removing the curse of involuntary servitude from his country, and, therefore, exerted himself by speech and writing to show the evils springing from it, and to induce Slaveholders to abandon it. Now many slaves were continually escaping into a border free state, and were wont to take the town of his residence in their route. As the citizen was known to hate Slavery, the masters of the fugitives held him in suspicion, and, by menaces, and scandal, made his home so unpleasant that he was compelled to change his residence. So he removed, also, to a free state, hoping to remain at rest. Presently after his removal, there occurred another flight of slaves, and, this man still lying under suspicion, the masters charged him with aiding and abetting in their escape. They therefore went to the Governor of their own State, and demanded that the citizen should be brought a prisoner from his new home, and put on trial for aiding in the escape of the fugitives, in the State from which he had removed.

And the Governor said: This is right, and your request is proper. Suspicion of aiding in the escape of slaves, when resting on a citizen of a free state, is sufficient ground for bringing him to trial, and, if necessary, thrusting him into prison among us. Our rights as Slaveholders are superior to the rights of Non-Slaveholders, and if citizens of a free state become suspected of interfering with them, that should at any time render those citizens the proper subjects for the control of our sheriffs. For non-slaveholding freemen are a class inferior to us. I will, therefore, command the Governor of the free state to surrender this preacher of freedom; and he will not dare to disobey, because the order issues from a slave state.

So he made an imperative requisition on the Governor of the free state to surrender the preacher.

Now the latter Governor was a good democrat, and stood in mortal fear of the order of Slaveholders, esteeming them a race of superior beings. When the requisition came, he received it with great reverence, as if an inspired writing from on high. And he said to himself: I have been long desiring an opportunity to pay my court to the Slave Power, and this requisition is the very thing which I could most desire. For, by obeying it, I shall at once vindicate my democratic principles, and gain favor with the proprietors of the nation. I see that the requisiton calls for one *suspected* of aiding fugitive slaves to escape. So much the better for me. If I can but succeed in establishing the principle, that the bare suspicion of aiding in these escapes should subject all citizens of free states to liability of trial and imprisonment on slave soil, I may gain as much renown as the man who robbed the People of their free territory in the name ot their own sovereignty. Besides, this rampant spirit of liberty, now so prevalent in our country, needs all the power of Democracy and Slavery combined to keep it in order; and I will make of this preacher an example of terror to all aiders of fugitive slaves.

So he issued an order to a sheriff to seize the preacher, and to deliver him up to trial and a prison in the slave state. But the preacher, secretly learning what the democratic Governor intended for him, fled to another free state, leaving his family behind him. There he continued an exile from family and home, under suspicion of aiding human beings to recover their natural rights, and in constant danger of imprisonment by reason of his love of liberty.

XXXIV.

THE DOUGHFACE'S LETTER.

Hospitality costs nothing, when the toil of Slaves pays the expense.

A Doughface, traveling in the South, took lodgings for a night at the mansion of a Slaveholder, where he so entertained his host by agreeable conversation, and his extreme servility, that the host requested him, as it was already late in autumn, to become his guest during the winter. The Doughface, thinking himself highly honored, was unable to resist the invitation, and accordingly arranged his affairs to remain. Domiciled as a member of the family, great parties were made for him, and he was introduced to all the neighboring planters. To add to the favor with which he was received by his new friends, he improved every opportunity to eulogize the system of Slavery. They, in return, so flattered and bepraised him, that his common sense was seriously impaired. In addition to this, his host, discovering how he could be most effectually wrought upon, ordered a slave to attend him constantly, to make his fires, black his boots, and saddle a horse for him whenever he wished. These tokens of regard soon completely upset him; for as he never before had been served by a slave, he became so intoxicated with the treatment, that he began to think Slavery altogether divine. And, to convert the whole North to his new faith, he wrote an article, and sent it to a national democratic paper for insertion. It was in these words:

MR. EDITOR:—I have never been so thoroughly convinced of the folly and fanaticism of the abolitionists, as during the few weeks of my stay here. I have been residing, for the past month, in the midst of hospitalities and delights, such as I had never before imagined. I am tarrying with a Slaveholder, whose heart is a perfect well of generosity! He thinks no kindness in his power to bestow, too great for me. He has given several parties on my account, and procured my invitation to several more given by his neighbors. He has set one slave to wait upon me; he has my boots cleaned by daybreak every morning; and a horse is kept for my especial pleasure. In addition to all this, he charges nothing for my board! Was such hospitality ever known in the North? I think not.

My host owns a hundred negroes. I need not say that they are happy. No pigs on any Northern farm are fatter and sleeker. They have abundance to eat, and as much clothing as this climate demands. We, who are good democrats, know that if a man's belly is well filled, and he has a pair of pantaloons and a shirt, he should aspire to nothing higher. Do you know of a democrat in this condition who does? Now my host's negroes have all these things. Should they ask for more?

They do not break up the families of the slaves in the South, as the mendacious abolitionists say. For marriage is made easy for them, and there are strictly speaking no families. Fathers do not know their own children; brothers and sisters do not know their relationship. Surely this is democratic. There is always, however, a sufficient mixture of white blood among the negroes to beautify them; and the mixed races seem to be gaining on both the pure colors.

When they sell a babe from its mother's arms, she feels badly for a time, but gets over it at last, and the good condition of the market for that commodity soon replaces the lost child. The best institutions have their vulnerable points, you know. Should Slavery be assailed on account of its distressing incidents?

Peace and good order prevail perpetually on this plantation. The slaves love their masters to distraction, and it is doubtful whether the inducements which might be offered by a world of abolitionists, could entice one from his service. He says he can confide in their honesty to any degree.

My host is a great admirer of the Fugitive Slave Law. He thinks it adds one more link to our glorious Union, and one to the leg of every slave, and that the general submission to it speaks well for the healthfnl tone of public and private morality prevalent in the North. He thinks that as soon as the People become too proud, or too obstinate to chase run-away negroes, the days of the pure democracy will be numbered, and our free institutions will go down in blood. These are my sentiments.

My host is in favor of Colonization. He says that the free negroes are a great pest about the plantations, because they incite the slaves to theft and robbery, and set the example of insubordination. They are themselves great thieves and robbers. He thinks that there are enough of this class in the South, could they be all removed at once to Africa, to Christianize that ill-fated land in a twelvemonth. He thinks Colonization should be promoted, also, because if the free North should once get a hankering for Amalgamation, and the national democrats start in a general race for it, the monopoly of the South in that business would be seriously encroached upon.

As to the Christian character of the slaves, so far as my observation extends, it is above all praise. The greater part of them belong to some Church; and laying out of view their lying, thieving, and licentious habits, which are nearly universal, they are very exemplary followers of the Cross!

Shall this beautiful system of social relations be rudely dissolved by fanaticism? Shall emancipation be suffered to destroy our free institutions? Shall we, by loosing the bonds of three millions of slaves, encourage an amalgamation voluntary on both sides, disperse all the free negroes waiting to be impressed into the Christianization of Africa, and banish from the world all these glorious hospitalities? Surely this is not democratic.

For my part, I shall adhere to the compromises

of the Constitution. I tremble at the thought of any other amalgamation than such as is patronized by Slaveholders; and, as a good democrat, I stand inexorably opposed to the extension of liberty any farther than they will sanction, or in any direction not pleasing to them.

When the Doughface had written this letter, he read it to his host, who expressed his decided approbation of it. Only he felt a delicacy in having any thing mentioned about his hospitality; because, said he, *the labor of our slaves pays the expense of our hospitality, and it costs us nothing.* We dislike to boast of it.

You need have no concern on that point, said his guest. There is such an exalted conception of Slaveholders' hospitality prevailing in the North, that none but fanatical abolitionists stop to inquire who endures the sacrifice that feeds it. Certainly, I never before dreamed that the slave could claim the honor of it, and even now I think there must be some way to credit it to the Slaveholder's account.

So the letter was sent into the North, and published, with editorial commendations. And the host and his guest flattered themselves that it would end all controversy about Slavery, wherever it might be read.

XXXV.

THE KITCHEN SLAVE.

Not every Southern Gentleman dares to bring all his Children into the parlor.

On the banks of a southern river, lived a Slaveholder noted for his hospitality, for whom a large plantation, and a multitude of toiling bondmen, made unbounded hospitality anything but a sacrifice. He lived in courtly splendor. A noble mansion sheltered his family, beautiful gardens and parks gratified his taste, carriages and horses were ready at his call, and troops of servants obeyed his command. He was a king in all but the name.

To the residence of this Slaveholder came a visitor from the North. He was kindly and politely received, and every attention was paid him, which it was in the power of southern chivalry to show. In particular did the host endeavor to make his guest understand how happy and contented were the slaves that thronged the plantation, and what mighty triumphs Christianity had gained among them.

Said the host: I not only instruct them in the precepts of our holy religion, but I try to set before them an attractive example in my own conduct.

As our laws wisely forbid teaching them to read, I cull out appropriate texts and chapters from the Bible, and read them in their hearing, and then comment upon them in language adapted to their capacities. I generally select such portions of Scripture as tend to make them satisfied with their condition, and such as beget a spirit of submission to the severer dispensations of Providence. When I desire to expand their minds, I read chapters like the first in Matthew, the eighth in first Chronicles, and similar ones, which are peculiarly adapted to the wants of servants, and not at all incendiary. In the cultivation of their moral sentiments, we labor under some disadvantages. As the institution is at bottom a patriarchate, certain features peculiar to the ancient models, must necessarily appear among us. Thus we expand the marriage relation at each end, making it both polygamic and polyandric—admitting the husband to have many wives, and likewise the wife to have many husbands. In this way we multiply our slaves at pleasure, and can sell the young without much injury to the feelings of the parent. We do not strictly break up families, because our slaves are not so much united in families, as in herds. But the marriage relation being thus liberal in its requirements, there is needed an astonishing amount of instruction and moral example on the part of the masters, to keep our property from multiplying faster than any patriarch's. Often, indeed, the master, struggling like a hero to restrict the too luxuriant growth of the polygamic institution, loses his foothold, and presents a moral example directly the reverse of what a rigid continence would demand. But through that happy system of compensation pervading nature, to atone for the master's incontinence, our plantations are sprinkled with a population whose features present proof at once of that master's great temptations, and of the most effulgent beauties of polygamy.

As the guest here hinted that this language was not altogether intelligible to him, the Slaveholder rose, and led him from the parlor to a kitchen at a little distance from the house, in which sat a little boy whose face bore an unmistakable resemblance to the master of the mansion, and in whose complexion were mingled the colors of two different races.

Gazing for a moment at the boy, the guest inquired why his host did not adopt him openly as a son, and admit him with his other children to the parlor.

If I had my pleasure in the matter, said the Slaveholder, I should do so; but ever since this boy first appeared, a strange sickness and decline seems to have afflicted my lady, and she is annoyed with the sight of him. She says little about the boy, but she hates him, and in some manner his presence is connected with her sickness, and I dare not bring him into the parlor, and so I keep him in the kitchen. Besides, though most of my neighbors, like myself, have children of this boy's complexion, we all feel a dislike to having them seen. For though they are valuable property as well as children, that peculiar sense of propriety which grows out of the prevalence of monogamic marriage, is in a degree outraged by their presence. Indeed, it is nothing but the consolation derived from the thought that we are imitating the patriarchs, and the prospect of converting such children into money, that could reconcile us to the inconvenience of rearing them on the same plantation with the pure white ones. However, the saints must expect trials in this world.

Before the northern guest could recover from his surprise at this speech, they returned to the parlor, when a little bell was rung, and the wife of the host entered with her children. Then the host closed the evening with devotional exercises.

XXXVI.

THE PRESIDENTIAL CATECHISM.

A Democratic Candidate for the Presidency should aim to establish and perpetuate Slaverv as a National Institution.

In the Great Republic, the People had become so servile, that instead of voting directly for him who was most worthy of the chief magistracy, they gave their suffrages for whomever their party leaders selected, however much they might dislike him, or even though they might think him incompetent to fill the office with dignity. This state of things had been brought about by the office-mongers, who managed to govern the People by dividing them into parties, and inspiring them with bitter animosities, so that a perpetual fear of being beaten by the opposite faction in the struggle for the public offices, made nearly every man in the land follow his leaders to sustain any measure however wrong, or however anti-democrat. When a candidate was brought forward, the People did not ask themselves: Is he a good man? Is the principle which he represents just and right? but they inquired: Did my party-leaders nominate him? If assured of this, they voted for him without hesitation, and never questioned the infallibility of their leaders.

The People being in this condition of bitter partisan antagonism, the Slaveholders with whom they had entered into a compact of union, took advantage of the party strife to subject them to entire servitude. Their method was this—to propose a measure to one party injurious to the liberties of the People, and if the party to which the measure was proposed, rejected it, they would then threaten secession to their opponents; and thus by alternately bribing and menacing both, they would compel the party-leaders step by step to adopt principles destructive of all liberty. By this process of discipline they had trained up a set of politicians so thoroughly indifferent to the welfare of the People as to scruple at nothing which the Slaveholders proposed, and who would not even bring out a candidate who had not first pledged himself to administer the government for the perpetuation, and greatest possible extension of Slavery.

While the People were thus submissive to their party-leaders, and these latter, to the Slaveholders, a convention assembled to nominate a candidate for the Presidency. And when all things were ready, the leaders in private conclave produced their expected nominee to have him examined by the proper judges of political merits.

Then a Slaveholder took a seat, and causing the aspirant for office to stand up before him read to him the National Catechism in these words:

Will you, if elected, do all in your power to make the Government an organ for Slaveholders rather than for the People?

Will you, if elected, endeavor to make Slavery a national institution by gradually thrusting it into the free states, and by perpetuating a Fugitive Slave Law?

Will you, if elected, enforce all the compromises of the Constitution which favor Slavery, and disregard those which favor the People?

Will you, if elected, appoint Slaveholders to so many of the principal offices, as to have the administration truly favorable to Slavery?

Will you, if elected, endeavor to rob the People of all their territory sacred to liberty, and in the name of Popular Sovereignty deliver it over to Slaveholders?

Will you, if elected, favor the extension of the Republic southward, but constantly oppose its extension northward?

Will you, if elected, connive at military expeditions for the purpose of first robbing foreign territory, and then subjecting it to Slavery?

Will you, if elected, favor the disbursing of public monies in the slaveholding section of the Union, and oppose as much as possible, their disbursement in the non-slaveholding section?

Will you, if elected, in case of a vacancy in the National Judiciary, appoint only the tried friends of Slavery to that important station?

Will you, if elected, do all these things in the name of Democracy?

Then the happy aspirant, straightening himself up, answered:

If the questions just proposed to me had been precepts instead of interrogatories, I should call them the very decalogue of Democracy. They are, at least, a safe chart for a democratic President. I rejoice to find myself among men who understand so well how to manage the People. It is not by doing the things which advance their welfare that one gains their confidence, but by pretending to democracy, and at the same time using them to overthrow their own liberties. Their proper position is that of servitude, and I should labor with unflagging zeal, if elected, to bring them to that condition. Of course, I would begin with extravagant professions of democracy, for under such professions the People would suspect nothing. Next I would favor the monopoly of the soil of the territories by Slaveholders; and then going on quietly, I would secure a judicial decision from the High Court of the nation, allowing a permanent residence of masters with their slaves within the bounds of the free states. To carry the first measure through, a steady cry of Popular Sovereignty would be needed for some time; and, in general, we might say, the more thoroughly outrageous our measures, the more prolonged and far-echoing should be our shouting for democracy. In the midst of such an infernal din as I would propose to make, the People would be compelled, through the sheer force of noise and confusion, to yield to our measures. Should they, however, become suspicious of us, we might occasionally raise terrific rumors of war to divert their attention; or perhaps we might actually plunge into a war with some nation that does not buy our cotton, or which is too weak to beat the People we ride. There would be magnificent laurels to be won in such a war, and their greenness would be exceedingly pleasant to behold, long after the return of peace. You will excuse my alluding to such an event, but I have a passion for laurels.

I need not assure you that to every one of the above questions, I answer decidedly in the affirmative. I have only to request that the interrogatories propounded to me, by an amendment of the Constitution, be required to be put to every candidate for the Presidency.

After hearing this favorable response, the Slaveholders gave their consent to his nomination, and the party-leaders hoisted him at once on the backs of the People.

XXXVII.

THE REVIVAL IN THE SOUTH.

In the South there are two Gospels preached; one for the Master, and the other for the Slave.

In the Church of the Hermitage there once occurred a great revival of religion. For a preacher, full of zeal for souls, and for the possessions of an heiress resident in the vicinity, came into the precinct, and by his eloquence drew crowds together from all quarters. And many planters came in carriages, bringing wives and daughters, and listened to the Gospel. And as the interest in the matter of their salvation grew stronger and deeper, many of the planters became converts, and rejoiced in the discovery of it. Day after day, the house resounded with the alternate weeping and shouting of the planters, and of their wives and children, and many prayers were put up which could be heard afar off. But while the planters and their families were thus intent upon their soul's salvation, and daily rejoicing in the ministrations of the word, the drivers of the carriages, who were slaves, sat without the house holding their horses, or played at marbles beneath the shade of the tulip-trees which grew about the church.

Now it chanced when the revival was at its height, that a Northern Stranger was passing the sanctuary, and hearing the loud prayers of the preacher, drew near to one of the doors, and looking in he saw the tears of the hearers, and heard their sobbing. Listening to the words of the preacher, he soon discovered that a great anxiety for salvation in the next world had occasioned the weeping. But looking out beneath the tulip-trees, he was astonished to see some of the slaves who had driven the carriages, engaged in lively sport with their marbles. For he thought from the interest manifested by the audience, that the slaves must be in imminent peril, being so unconcerned. The more he considered the matter, the more he was perplexed; when stepping up to one standing like himself without the door, but who appeared too poorly clad to be the owner of any of the slaves, he asked the reason why the anxiety for salvation did not get out beneath the tulip-trees. Then the non-slaveholder said: I clearly see, O stranger, that you are not acquainted with our manners and customs, and that you notice many things which a native would never observe. Every Sunday, and in the times of a revival, may slaves be seen here, either at play with their marbles, or holding their horses, while their masters are within listening to the word. But it attracts little attention, for the custom has nothing singular in it to us. The reason of it is this: We have among us two Gospels, one for the masters, and another for the slaves. At least, I think it must be so. For whenever a preacher comes here, he is sure to set the Gospel net for the masters first, and then for the slaves; whether it is because they are the greatest sinners, or only the richest, it is hard to tell. After the masters have been pretty well harried, they turn to the slaves and preach a Gospel which is comprised in a single precept: *Servants obey your masters.* And as conformity to this precept is thought all-sufficient for their salvation, the preachers generally allow the slaves at this church to play at marbles, while they occupy themselves with the more laborious task of saving their owners.

By which Gospel do you expect to be saved yourself? said the Stranger.

Indeed, replied the other laughing, I hardly know. Belonging to neither class, we who hold no slaves must await, methinks, the preaching of a new Gospel, or, if we enter heaven at all, must try to wring in with the slaves, by the operation of some celestial three-fifths rule, which will let in fellows who have no just title. For I hear that a good part of our Slaveholders enter Congress that way, and expect to enter glory by a similar rule. But if you wish to know why the master's Gospel is not preached to the slaves, you would better inquire of the preacher himself.

So the Stranger waited till the congregation was dismissed, and taking the preacher aside, he inquired why he was not as zealous for the salvation of the slaves without the door, as for their masters who sat within.

Then said the Preacher: We cannot preach the

Gospel which commands all men to love one another as brethren, to masters and slaves together. For do you not see that such a Gospel would destroy the master's authority, making the master a brother of the slave, and the slave an equal of his master? We therefore accomodate it to the tastes of the masters, and give it such a coloring that it may not in the least prejudice the relation between them. So we tell the master, that if he is not baptized, and does not repent, and join the Church, he must be damned; but we do not tell him that he will be damned, if he does not treat his slave as a brother. Most of us preachers who own no slaves, know this to be true, but we do hate to say so; while the slaveholding preachers have forgotten that it is true. And, therefore, the Gospel we preach is a little different from what it was when it was in the keeping of the Apostles. But we get along very smoothly with ours. For with it, we get a full church and a well supported ministry. It seems to me, that when the alternative lies between preaching a diluted Gospel to a full church, and the pure Gospel to a small one, we should choose the large church and the diluted Gospel. Having thus provided the masters with spiritual food, we have but one word left for the slave —Obedience. We teach that his only path to heaven lies through entire submission to his master.

You see, therefore, why we feel no concern for these slaves here without the door. They do not constitute the Church which we aspire to build up. Their salvation is not of much consequence to us, nor to the Lord's kingdom, as we understand it.

When the Northern Stranger had heard this explanation, he mounted his horse, and returning to the highway, resumed his journey, wondering within himself whether there is any limit to man's capacity for hypocrisy. But the preacher continued the revival, till he had converted most of the neighboring planters, and finally became converted himself, into a master on the plantation of the beautiful heiress, where he applied the precepts of the Gospel in the most novel manner.

XXXVIII.

THE SORE THROAT.

Democratic Senators do not prosper by speaking the Truth.

A MEMBER of the American Senate, distinguished for his talent and servility to the Slave Power, though not marked for his corporeal bulk, was seized, during a recess of Congress, with a purulent sore throat, which affected his tongue, and became so violent a disease as to require the attendance of several physicians. Each examined the mouth and throat to see, if possible, what had been the cause of the soreness, and to remove it by an application of the proper remedies. One expressed his opinion as to the cause, and another gave a different explanation, and still another differed from the rest, and they were very much perplexed, both with the disease itself and with their own disagreements about its cause.

But after the Senator had heard all their explanations, he very naively asked them whether *lying* ever brought on the sore throat. And when they answered that they had read of many causes for that disease, but had never suspected that lying could produce it, the Senator said:

Nevertheless, I imagine that is the real cause of my sickness. You probably know, gentleman, that I am very much in want of the Presidency. I have been aiming for it ever since I came into political life. But as I perceived that the only way to reach that high office was by courting the favor of those who had it in their gift, I fell to advocating the measures of the Slaveholders. Now their plans cannot succeed by a public advocacy unless the advocate become a vigorous liar. So as soon as I saw what was requisite to my success, I set about the cultivation of lying as an art, and I have attained in it an unexpected proficiency. But, singular as it may seem, from the very first day in which I commenced my career till now, I have not produced a single round and plump lie, that has not been followed by an attack of sore throat. And even my slight mis-representations, have brought on the same complaint. I know that I am right, for the two things have so long happened together, that I know there must be some connection of cause and effect between them, and you need not attempt to convince me to the contrary. But just give me a remedy which may reach a disease produced by so singular a cause.

Then answered one of the physicians, smiling: If the case is as you say, and if lying is the real cause of your disease, why not try speaking the truth? That would be the allopathic remedy.

Ah, gentlemen, said the Senator, in such a case as this I should prefer the homœopathic practice, *minus* the small doses. How can you recommend to me in the present aspect of my political fortunes to speak the truth? Am I not a democratic Senator? Was I not chief actor in the robbery of the People of their Great Territory? And can that grand scheme of exalting the Slave Power above the People succeed fully, without further fraud and lying? Certainly not. But even my ordinary duties as democratic statesman forbid an abandonment of my high art in which I have acquired so much skill. To lead the portion of the People with whom I act, the most refined and persistent lying is a matter of necessity. Lies are the staple of their knowledge—lies about every thing—lies about the heavens—lies about the earth—lies about the things under the earth—and above all, lies about their leaders' political doings, which belong neither to heaven nor earth, are incessantly and clamorously demanded. You know not what it is to be a democratic statesman. Then to crown all, I don't love the truth any too well in my natural condition. And if lying has made my throat sore, would not an attempt to speak the truth prove absolutely fatal to me? I know it would be fatal to my political prospects. No, gentlemen; speaking the truth cannot cure my disease.

Upon hearing this, the physicians macerated the worthy Senator's second Kansas Bill, and making it into a poultice bound it about his neck. And, wearing this for a few days, he entirely recovered, being cured by the principle—*similia similibus.*

XXXIX.

THE DOUGHFACE APPROVED.

A Doughface aspires to nothing higher than the approbation of a Slaveholder

A Doughface who lived on the bank of the beautiful river which separates certain slave states ot the Great Republic from others that are free, on account of suspicions that had been cast on the purity of his democracy, became very much concerned to have it put to a trial, and stamped with approbation by a competent judge. So entering a light canoe he rowed across the river to the residence of a Slaveholder, whom he considered quite adequate to examine him, and whose public approval he knew would remove all doubts from his own mind, and make him pass current as a genuine democrat wherever he might go. When he had announced the object of his visit, the Slaveholder complimented him highly, and taking him to a tavern near by, gave him somewhat wherewith to strengthen his resolution, and in the presence of a crowd of by-standers they sat down to the examination.

In order, said the Slaveholder, that I may test your democracy in the best possible manner, it will be necessary for you to respond to a few interrogatories. Your answers will bring out your democratic virtue, as the questions I intend to propose are general, and smack of nationality.

Said the Slaveholder: Do you know why you are a democrat?

The Doughface answered: I do not. I never make it a practice to understand the reason of my political action. I am connected with my party by a kind of instinct, and natural sympathy with every thing mean and base. It is not natural for a democrat to be governed by reason in acting with his party. It is enough for him to follow where others lead.

Said the Slaveholder: Do you ever doubt the honesty of your party-leaders?

Never, said the Doughface. The honesty and patriotism of our party-leaders are considered by ordinary democrats, a matter which can never be questioned.

Said the Slaveholder: What do you understand by patriotism?

The Doughface answered: I have no very definite ideas about it, but as far as I can understand, patriotism is devotion to the party and the party-leaders, right or wrong.

Then the Slaveholder asked: What do you understand by the terms *liberty* and *democracy?*

The Doughface replied: I understand by *liberty*, the privilege of a few men to govern and own large masses of their fellow-beings; and by *democracy*, the support of such liberty by party organizations.

What do you understand, said the Slaveholder, by the terms *Justice* and *Truth?*

Said the Doughface: The words convey no meaning to my mind.

Said the Slaveholder. What do you understand by Popular Sovereignty?

The Doughface answered: It is the government of Non-Slaveholders in one community, by the Slaveholders in another.

Then the Slaveholder asked: Do you believe men like me to be the highest style of man?

I do, said the Doughface.

Said the Slaveholder: Do you believe the government of the Union should always be in our keeping?

I do, said the Doughface.

Said the Slaveholder: Do you approve of extending the area of Freedom?

I do, said the Doughface, if it be not extended northward; and if Slavery can be introduced into territory where it has never been, and not endangered where it already exists.

Then asked the Slaveholder: Is there any measure which Slaveholders can propose, which you would not submit to, if your party-leaders gave it their sanction?

None whatever, said the Doughface; his party-leaders' approval of a measure, is always a good democrat's final reason to approve the same thing.

Do you feel it an honor, said the questioner, to be politically allied with Slaveholders, and to have them for your party-leaders?

I do, said the Doughface; I feel it to be the greatest of honors.

Would you pursue for us our fugitive slaves, said the questioner, wherever blood-hounds are scarce?

With alacrity, said the Doughface.

If Non-Slaveholders, said the other, should endeavor to combine in order to restrict our control of the People and our Slaves, what would you do?

Said the Doughface: I would point them to their constitutional obligations, tell them of the danger of a dissolution of the Union, and cry democracy at the top of my voice.

Do you believe, said the Slaveholder, in Polygamy, and Involuntary Amalgamation as national institutions.

Save Democracy, said the Doughface, I believe in nothing else.

Then the Slaveholder, taking the Doughface by the hand, made him stand on his feet, and turning to the by-standers, he said: Here is a Democrat approved. He knows nothing of Justice and Truth; he swears by the last word of his party-leaders; he believes in a liberty limited by Slavery, and a democracy in which the many are governed by the few; in a Popular Sovereignty in which non-slaveholding communities are governed by Slaveholders; in Polygamy and Involuntary Amalgamation as national institutions; and he professes himself ready to hunt our fugitive slaves. What more could be demanded of him? It is by the aid of such creatures as this, that we govern both slaves and the People. May his race be numerous, and long-lived! May they multiply like the lice of Egypt! Once more, in the presence of you all, I pronounce him a genuine democrat.

Then the by-standers arose and led him to the bank of the river. And the Doughface descending into his light canoe, paddled home again, rejoicing that after so thorough and public an examination, there could be no further doubt of his democracy.

THE PURIFIED MAIL BAGS.

XL.

THE PURIFIED MAIL BAGS.

The passage of Anti-Slavery papers through a Slave State is dangerous to free institutions.

In a slave state of the Model Republic there was a town whose inhabitants were zealous above measure in perpetuating human bondage. They labored for nothing so much as the extension of it to the virgin territories of the Republic, and they were ever on the alert to discover dangers to the institution. Through this place there passed weekly the national mail, bearing its wonted burden of letters and papers. But it had become an object of extreme terror to these guardians of Slavery, as they believed that incendiary documents often passed in it. Some of their leaders therefore wrote to the chief Master of the Posts, and stated their fears, and the imminent danger to the country from the transit of matter so combustible. He wrote in reply as follows:

You did well to write me on a subject of such grave importance. I have myself been greatly exercised at the thought of the risk to which our free institutions are exposed by the contagious presence of anti-slavery papers, and their general circulation. I see danger in all documents of that kind. It is not so much from the slaves that the danger is to be feared, as from our white non-slaveholding population. The institutions of the South rest as truly on their backs, as on the backs of our slaves. But they do not know it. They think it an honor and an advantage to themselves as yet, to aid us in holding our human property in servitude. But they are themselves impoverished by the system, and reduced nearly to the level of slaves. Now this truth, the anti-slavery papers and documents which pass to and fro in the mail, are constantly declaring and explaining. If these documents, therefore, should obtain circulation among our Non-Slaveholders, we, who at present control them and our slaves together, would find our power speedily shaken. For discovering Slavery to be prejudicial to them, they would at once apply the torch of emancipation, and the edifice of our own freedom would soon be in a conflagration which nothing could extinguish. Slave-breeding, Concubinage, and Amalgamation, which are the jewels of our free institutions, would soon disappear, and there would be nothing left among us but Justice and Equal Rights. Can a Slaveholder look forward to such results with any feelings but those ot horror and alarm? There is nothing we have so much to dread as the triumph of Justice and Truth. May the Lord save us from anything of the kind!

But that I may do my duty to prevent these consequences, I hereby authorize all Post-Masters to open the mails, and take from them all incendiary matter, by which I mean, all matter bringing in question the right of slaveholding. It is well enough for northern people to pay most of our postage, and keep up the postal system for us, but it is not well that they should send through the South anti-slavery papers. A single one might be the occasion of suddenly revealing to our non-slaveholding population their true position, and thus endangering our power, or it might open the way to Canada, to hundreds of our servants.

Please, therefore, to keep a careful watch of the mails, and suffer none of this incendiary matter to circulate in the South, lest her chivalrous sons awake some sunny morning, and find themselves surrounded by thousands of emancipated slaves, the wrecks of our glorious Union! I write under most painful apprehensions.

Now when this missive was received, a crowd gathered upon the arrival of the next mail, and seizing the bags they carried them forth into a public square, and emptying them they found two doubtful documents, which were opened and read in the hearing of all. And one proved to be a little pamphlet by the American Tract Society. This was carefully replaced in the mail, for there was nothing in it they thought tending to establish Justice. The other was a printed copy of the Declaration of Independence, which was also read as far as these words: We hold these truths to be self-evident, that all men are created equal, and are possessed of certain inalienable rights—when the crowd shouted at once: That is an abolition paper!

Then taking it out they kindled a great fire, and with loud cries and rejoicings burned it to ashes.

So the mail-bags were purified, and that night the crowd slept soundly, for the Union had been saved.

XLI.

THE DISTRESSED SEMINARY.

Slaves may be sold to support the Gospel.

THE directors of a Theological Seminary in the South, founded for the spread of the Gospel of peace and love, were wont to loan its funds in such a way as to bring in a sure annual income to its corps of teachers. And as the best security in that region for money loaned was slaves, they lent a portion of the funds of the institution on a mortgage of eight human beings. Time passed, and the borrower, being unsuccessful in business, was unable either to pay the interest or restore the principal. The directors of the Seminary, perceiving the state of affairs, held a council to decide upon the action necessary to pursue; for they began to fear that there might be an utter loss of the money, unless they had recourse to the law. Then one of them who had much experience in such matters gave this advice:

Our Seminary, brethren, was founded for the spread of the Gospel. But the Gospel cannot be proclaimed unless teachers be instructed, and a ministry be supported to divide the word rightly, and in accordance with the standard set by the

Apostles. Now a ministry must be prepared by theological training, for the preachers of the word cannot, as in the days of the Apostles, receive inspiration directly from God, as he has now no direct contact with the human intellect. And, therefore, theological seminaries are founded to supply the want of inspiration, and by a sifting of the letter of Scripture, to discover the only right path to salvation. For the Gospel is not now so much a proclamation of glad tidings, as a gloomy message touching the awful hazards to which one is exposed after death by simply being born a man; and its function is to awaken men to a due sense of their danger from God.

To raise up preachers of such a Gospel is the object of our Seminary. But we cannot instruct and prepare preachers, unless the revenue of the Seminary is steadily supplied. The stream of money must be constant, or our Gospel will not be preached. The means of grace are not divine influences alone, but a little money likewise. Do you not see what is our duty in the present emergency? Our creditor cannot pay, but we have a mortgage on eight of his slaves. It is clear that the slaves should be sold at auction. And though by so doing we sacrifice the slaves, we do it to subserve the necessities of the preached word. This is perfectly right. For see how the case stands. No money regularly paid in, there is no longer any theological seminary; if no seminary of theology, no Gospel preachers; no preachers, no salvation of the world. My heart bleeds, brethren, when I think of a world lying in wickedness, and of the heathen in foreign lands who are going down annually to perdition by the million! I am not so much distressed for our own heathen, for I know that for every soul of them lost, there are many bales of cotton saved to our planters; and perhaps the making of the cotton will be counted to them for righteousness. But as for those foreign heathen, they are in imminent danger of falling into the hands of God. Now as it was to prevent this danger, that we are permitted to be stewards of the Gospel, a faithful stewardship and the wants of our Seminary command a public sale. There seems to me, too, a beautiful dispensation of Providence here, in the bare fact of our selling our own heathen for the redemption of those abroad. What an affecting tale, also, will our missionaries be able to relate to those distant heathen, that they could never have been preachers, had not the liberty and happiness of eight human beings been sacrificed for life, in order to equip them for their mission. This simple story would give them a very vivid sense of the worth and costliness of the Gospel, and of the overwhelming necessity of an application of its grace to their souls.

Then another of the directors said: Never before have I had so clear an illustration of the things which it is lawful to do, to sustain the Gospel, and I never understood till now, how it is that good is brought out of evil.

New truths, said the former, are always being revealed to the minds of the saints.

Now after they had taken counsel together, as is above related, the directors voted unanimously that the mortgage should be foreclosed. So the slaves were sold, and the money went into the treasury of the Seminary.

XLII.

THE RESTITUTION.

The Union will indemnify the Slaveholder against the loss of unborn Slave Babies.

In a southern state, during the revolution which severed the united colonies from the mother country, many Slaveholders lost valuable property; some lost horses; some, oxen; others, slaves. Long after the revolution, and after the establishment of a union between the Slaveholders and the People, the descendants of those sufferers finding the Government very pliant in satisfying the demands of the ruling party to the Union, petitioned the national Congress for indemnification for losses sustained by their ancestors through the depredations of Indians. Now the Union owed the descendants of the predatory Indians certain monies. To do justice, therefore, and to pay Slaveholders for the losses of their dead fathers, the functionaries appointed by Congress withheld from the living Indians a sum sufficient, as they thought, to satisfy the claimants. But when the Government came to settle with these claimants, it was found that their demands did not amount, by many thousands of dollars, to the sum reserved to pay them. As, however, the ancestors of the petitioners had lost female slaves, a method was discovered by which their claims could be made to swell so as to cover the whole sum reserved. And an admirable document preserved in the archives of Congress, sets forth in brief terms this general method of expanding Slaveholders' claims. It reads in this wise:

It is not usual for your honorable body to count birds, and appraise their value, before they are hatched. But there are cases in which an estimate of this kind should be made in order to perpetuate our free institutions, and keep alive a sound democracy. If a Slaveholder possesses a parturient female slave, he no longer regards the adage which would dissuade from counting unhatched birds, as either wise or witty. Indeed, he counts upon birds from the very moment such property comes under his control. Standing in no childish fear of amalgamation, his calculations upon an increase of property so seldom fail, that the adage mentioned is in general discredit throughout the slaveholding region. We not only set a price on the babe that is born, but upon abstract and barely possible ones. These possibilities, like railroad stocks, have a market price which can be estimated with as much certainty as any other species of securities. Your honorable body should recollect that we, the flower of American Nobility, not only traffic in live babies, but in these possible ones, which are a kind of incorporeal hereditament; and as we are patrons of Polygamy and Concubinage, you can easily imagine how it is that our calculations regarding unhatched birds seldom fail. We give our profoundest studies to the subject of *possible*, *personal*, *real*, and *mixed* property; and we can show abundance of samples under each kind. In computing the value of a parturient slave, therefore, we add to the value of the mother that of her possible offspring, and the sum is her market price.

In the case of the claimants whose petition is now before us, there was a loss by their ancestors of parturient slaves. Those ancestors, therefore, lost a great number of possible, unborn babies; and if the ancestors were entitled to this species of property, surely their descendants should be indemnified for the loss.

We would recommend that a computation of the value of these possible babies be made, and that the sum with interest be paid to the petitioners. By so doing we not only do justice to them, but we establish a great and beneficent principle as a rule of national action, to wit, that the *Government will always indemnify Slaveholders for the unborn slave babies lost by their ancestors in war, whenever it can be done by appropriating to that end monies due Indians.* We know of no rule for political action so brilliantly just, or so thoroughly democratic. The setting a market value on our unborn children, is a spectacle which must inevitably attract the admiration of the world, and must give to democratic principles an impetus which no language can describe.

As to the Indians to whom this *balance* would

belong if the loss of *actual* property were alone taken into account, we think that in comparison with the restitution of unborn, and barely possible babies, to the heirs of their original owners, all rights to real property of any description, sink into absolute insignificance. Besides, neither Justice, nor Democracy requires any very nice regard from Congress to the rights of an Indian, or a Negro. Absolute justice, and democracy without alloy concern only the Anglo-Saxon white Slaveholder.

Your committee would recommend that the original claim of these petitioners to indemnification for the losses of their ancestors, be so far expanded on the basis of their title to unborn babies, as to include the surplus, which, on principles of vulgar justice would naturally belong to the Indians, and for which they may some day petition.

When Congress had heard this lucid report, being mostly from the North, they were entirely overcome by its logic, and promptly passed a bill granting the claim of the petitioners.

XLIII.

THE DOUGHFACE RELIEVED.

American Democracy prefers Involuntary to Voluntary Amalgamation.

A PROFESSED Democrat in a public house near the borders of the free states, was inveighing against the Abolitionists, and enumerating to the astonished by-standers their projects against liberty, and the evil things which they encouraged.

Said he: There is one practice which the Abolitionists advocate and sanction, which is most monstrous, I mean—Amalgamation. They are aiming to make this whole people a mongrel nation, in which neither a pure white nor a pure black can be found. To bring this about, they would legalize marriage between the two races. Now if this relation between the races were sanctioned by custom, that divinely implanted prejudice against the black color and the African, which from the foundation of the world the Deity designed should grace the moral character of the North American Anglo-Saxon, would soon disappear, and the affinities between white and black would become so strong as utterly to abolish marriages of whites with whites, and blacks with blacks. Then we should see whole platoons of white ladies marching South in search of colored gentlemen, and regiments of white gentlemen ransacking every southern kitchen in quest of colored women. I need not say what violent heart-burnings, jealousies, and dissensions between North and South would burst forth when such things shall occur! But in addition to all this, we all know, on the testimony of distinguished ethnologists, that an antipathy so murderous naturally exists between the two races, that if both were free, they could not form one community without incessant war and bloodshed. Who does not see now that if the marriage tie were once legalized between them, this murderous antipathy would suddenly vanish in a perfect *tohu vabohu* of connubial felicity and universal amalgamation? I am tortured with awful apprehensions in view of these probable results.

Then a Slaveholder, sitting by, said to the Democrat: I am surprised to find such candor, and such an example of clear prophetic vision in a Non-Slaveholder. But as you are a professed democrat, you are able to appreciate arguments tending to relieve the apprehensions you have just expressed, which ordinary men could not understand. One who is capable of following the fortunes of what now passes in America for Democracy, should be considered a man of most remarkable qualities, both of sense and resolution.

I think there is no danger of Amalgamation becoming general, for this reason: It is, at present, *involuntary* with one of the parties. If it were *voluntary with both*, there would of course be *less* than there is under the involuntary system. But where this latter prevails, it genders a practice of concubinage such as existed among the patriarchs, and thus limits the entire institution of Amalgamation to the control of a few masters of families. Thus we, the order of Slaveholders, have a kind of monopoly in this business, which we enjoy for the benefit of the community. It is a privilege, you perceive, which should be allowed only to a few—to men of a patriarchal mould, if I may so speak. Do you not also perceive that we, as permanent guardians of so valuable a privilege are the best of democrats? We not only prevent its becoming general, but we multiply laborers at pleasure. A model Slaveholder, one who might have associated with the patriarchs on equal terms, never needs go beyond his own plantation for laborers. They are mostly of home manufacture. We of course desire to keep this manufacture a monopoly, as we know how to carry it on with discretion. We, however, desire the People to give us all their unoccupied territory, as the business requires a very extensive field for the full development of all its perfections. There are latent beauties in it which none but Slaveholders can well understand.

Then the Democrat said: I feel very much relieved. I knew there was something terrible in Amalgamation beside the consequences of it, but I did not know what it was. I now perceive that it is the Amalgamation which is voluntary *on both sides*, which a good democrat should abhor; and though Involuntary Amalgamation goes on at a more rapid rate than the other, it ends only in multiplying laborers that can be sold. They, therefore, who preside over the institution of Involuntary Amalgamation seem to me the best of democrats, because they save us from voluntary Amalgamation, and constantly augment the public wealth. Yes; the mingling of the races is not a bad thing on these conditions, and the more I think of it, the more it seems to me I should like to be a patriarch myself.

And if you were, said the Slaveholder, you would differ little from what you are, save in your privileges, and that your democracy would take on additional lustre.

So saying he left the house, and the bystanders gazed after him with reverence and admiration, as a being belonging to a higher sphere than them selves.

XLIV.

THE CAPTURED FUGITIVE AND THE MINISTERS.

A Clergyman in regular standing in the Churches cannot pray publicly for the Freedom of a Fugitive Slave.

A SLAVE sat in prison not far from the monument of Bunker Hill, and wishing to be free from bondage, he sent a messenger to request of the Clergy of the city in which his prison was, to pray that he might be set at liberty; but if that might not be, that he might at least bear his afflictions patiently.

And the messenger went first to a Bishop, whom he found seated in a richly furnished study, reading the Missionary Herald. And the Bishop saluted him graciously, and gave him a seat. And as the messenger beheld what the Bishop was reading, he asked what tidings he found.

Good tidings, said the Bishop. For the souls of the heathen are saved in vast numbers, and the Church of the Lord receives daily increase in foreign lands.

We have a soul in prison who asks your prayers in the church on the morrow, that he too may be saved, said the messenger.

Poor soul, said the Bishop, with a sigh. What is his crime?

His crime is two-fold, said the messenger. He is black, and he is a fugitive slave.

I cannot pray for him, said the Bishop. I preach Christ and him crucified. My business is with the Gospel, and not with fugitive slaves.

And the holy man turned with indignation to the Missionary Herald, to read over again the list of the saved in the South Sea islands.

The messenger went his way, wondering whether it would not be well to preach Christ in the person of the slave crucified between the North and the South.

He next visited the minister of an evangelical Church, asking his prayers for the slave, as he had before asked those of the Bishop. And the minister looked musingly in his face for a moment, and then said sharply: I do not pray for slaves, unless it be that they may obey their masters.

So the messenger went his way; and trusting in the righteousness of his cause he called on still another clergyman of unexceptionable orthodoxy, and made known to him the slave's wishes. But this latter turning to him said: I would pray for Anthony with pleasure; but I have just come among this people, and I know not how they stand in this matter.

Pray, then, said the messenger, that strength be given him to bear his bondage patiently.

I dare not, replied the minister.

Then verily, said the other, you have need of the bondman's prayers, for surely you are a greater slave than he.

The messenger said to himself, as the door of the minister's house closed hastily after him: Has God deserted the land that no one can pray to him in behalf of the slave? But at last he remembered an Infidel who preached the Gospel of Humanity, and he wondered if he would dare pray for the captive, and if the Lord would listen to an Infidel's supplications. So he went forthwith to the Infidel Preacher, and asked him if he would lift up his voice in public prayer for the bondman.

And the Preacher said: As I hope for mercy, I will ask it for Anthony.

And when he gathered with his hearers to worship the God of Humanity, he prayed aloud and publicly that the fugitive slave might be made free. And all the People said, Amen.

And the God of Humanity, who rules alike the atoms and the worlds, heard his prayer, and loosed the bondman's chain.

XLV.

THE FUGITIVE CHURCH-MEMBER.

In the South, Church-members will run away from the means of Grace.

A SLAVE on a southern plantation becoming weary with bondage, and having his soul awakened to the blessings of liberty, seized the favorable moment, and made his escape to a northern free state. But his master coming in pursuit of him, with the aid of a detachment from the army and navy of the Union, took him captive once more, and the slave returned with a heavy heart to his first servitude. The master, however, fearing lest his servant should again escape, sold him to friends in the North, who gave money for his ransom, and he became at last, after much tribulation, a free man. Now the slave had been a member of a church, such as exists in the South, where the more favored and distinguished saints in the body of Christ, hold the more humble as property. Wishing for an honorable separation from his church, the emancipated bondman wrote to his brethren for a letter of dismissal and recommendation, that he might enter another church in the home of his adoption. But when his request reached its destination, it excited great indignation in the bosom of his former pastor, and in the hearts of the brethren. And they unanimously refused his request, and the pastor wrote back in reply as follows:

To ANTHONY:—Your impudence and sinfulness in asking an honorable dismissal from our church, of which you were once a member, is without a parallel in ecclesiastical annals. Whoever heard before of a fugitive servant asking for an honorable dismission from the church from which he has run away? Have you so ill learned Christ as to think that a fugitive from his master's service can be looked upon by him with approbation? Why, Christ came into the world to establish a Reign ot Love—a true Brotherhood. And how can there be a brotherhood among men unless the laws of true social order be observed? We all have our functions as members of Christ's body. Some must be feet; some, hands; and some, heads. The heads should own the feet and hands. Your earthly master was a head, and you were a foot. You both belonged to the body of Christ under this relation, and you both understood it. But what do I behold? The foot becomes dissatisfied and runs away from the head, and nothing can restore the foot to its proper connection, but the army and navy of our glorious Union! Nothing can keep the members of our church in unity but the strong arm of the government!

Have I labored with you so long to no purpose? Have I not instructed you over and over again, that you belong to the race of Ham and Canaan, and that the Divine curse resting upon you as such, appropriates you to a master forever? Have I not shown you that all the patriarchs owned servants? Have I not shown you from the words of the apostles that servants should obey their masters in all things? But notwithstanding all these means of grace, so freely bestowed, you ran away! Who now will teach you the pure precepts of the Gospel? Who now will read to you about Ham and Canaan, of the Patriarchs, and the Epistle to Philemon? When the Judge comes to make up his jewels, I expect to see no Anthony among them—only Anthony's former brethren in this church, his master, and some United States marshals! We shall have all the glory to ourselves, Anthony, and you will be alone in yours!

We can give you nothing but an excommunication. We think you deserve it, and we do not wish your former companions to understand that there is any forgiveness for sins like that of running away from one's master. For if they thought it a venial offense, whole churches would run away, and the means of grace would soon among us find no recipients. But we are not disposed to let the carnal man escape so easily. If he will not receive the grace voluntarily, he must be caught and held, and receive it on the bare back! And that it may come to you in this fashion, is the earnest prayer of

YOUR FORMER PASTOR AND BRETHREN.

XLVI.

THE EMANCIPATED DOUGHFACE.

Even a Doughface might become a lover of Liberty, if made a Slave himself.

An Anglo-Saxon, white Democrat, who talked much of his love of liberty, but who always managed to vote in such a way as to give the lie to his professions, desirous of trading in foreign lands, took ship and went abroad on the high seas. He had not voyaged far, before he was taken by a pirate, his vessel pillaged and sunk, and the crew, with himself and his fellow-passengers, made captives, and carried slaves to a barbarous nation, where, being put up at public auction, they were sold to the highest bidder. The Democrat himself fell to a purchaser uncommonly severe, who by dint of formidable tasks, and many a terrible flogging, finally kindled in his slave a lively sense of the value of universal liberty; in fact, made him a convert to what would be considered in the bondman's native country, the rankest political heresies. For misfortune sometimes convinces men of the worth of despised truths.

Thus, to a fellow-slave, who inquired whether it

were lawful for them to escape from servitude by flight, he answered:

When I was in my own country, I was very much degraded, even below what I am now. For I was a slave without knowing it. Living in what is called a free land, I was the member of a party whose leaders made me uphold just such slavery as we suffer here, under the pretence that my country's necessities required it. But alas! I knew nothing of the curse of bondage by experience. By my vote I aided to fasten on others the wretchedness we endure. I knew not what I did. I thought all things would go well if I but followed my leaders wherever they led. Many now suffer slavery in my native land, because my fellows fastened their chains. For the party-leaders used us to strengthen the bondage of millions, and open the way for the subjection of millions more.

Is it lawful for us to escape? It cannot be otherwise. No man can rightfully make property of us. We are not things, but persons, and Justice cries aloud against our enslavement. Not for an instant can the tyrant who oppresses us lawfully claim our obedience. The slave's right to freedom begins *now*, not to-day, nor to-morrow. His right to flee from servitude began the very moment he became a slave. Do we not see these things to be self-evident? Instant emancipation is our right; the effort to make it real, our instant duty. Not only *may* we run away, we *ought* so to do; and at the first opportunity I shall make my escape. No sophistry can convince me that I am bound to remain here.

But when endeavoring to put this good resolution in practice, he was caught by a native of a country in alliance with his oppressors, who was about to return him to his master. And the Democrat pleaded lustily for deliverance.

Now his captor was deeply impressed with his obligations to the government of which he was a subject, and he said:

My nation is in alliance with the nation of your master, and one article of our alliance is, that the fugitive slaves of the nation among whom you now are, shall be restored by us, if they take refuge here. We should violate a most solemn covenant, if I were to suffer you to run at large, as well as endanger the alliance.

The Democrat replied:

Any agreement between sovereign states which stipulates for a violation of the natural rights of man, is itself diabolical, and deserves prompt and constant disobedience from the subjects of either state. Civil laws and compacts derive all their rectitude and moral validity from the eternal Law of Right, and that Law ordains the equal freedom of all men, annulling involuntary servitude in all times and places. Will you obey the Law of Right which God himself is pledged to execute, or the transient statutes of men which conflict with that Law?

His captor answered:

The ordinance which compels me to return you to bondage, must be just. It was modeled after a similar one which was ordained by the allied states of a Christian nation beyond the Atlantic; and Christian nations never enact anything wrong into statutes.

You should not suppose, said the Democrat, that Christian nations always enact what is right. For they are sometimes infested with rotten democracies, out of whose carcasses swarm multitudes of foul legislators, who love nothing so well as the bondage of their fellows. And when these creatures crawl into the high places of Christian nations, you would think hell itself had vomited forth its foulest things, such monstrous statutes get enacted.

And is that the case, said the captor, with the Christian nation of which I spoke?

It is, said the Democrat. Just now the fair face of Liberty is disfigured with the ordinances of a rotten democracy, and the streams of Justice in that country are all running backward. Do not suppose that because a law restoring fugitives to bondage just now disfigures her statute book, that it is just, or that her People love it.

You might go free, said the captor, if I were not in doubt whether any law enacted by sovereign states be not obligatory upon their subjects, whatever be ordained.

Said the Democrat: Civil governments do not make Right. But they are bound to enact it. Now when a plain and palpable wrong is made law, it should be met by a blunt and uncompromising disobedience. For it is better that civil governments explode, than that rank injustice be permanently established among men.

Then *go*, said his captor.

So the Democrat fled. And when he reached his native land, he labored for nothing so much as the triumph of Liberty and Justice; nor could any rotten democracy deceive him more.

XLVII.

THE ORGAN FOR COLORS.

Slaveholders feel no repugnance to Amalgamation.

A DISPUTE arose between a Doughface and a Slaveholder as to the capacity of each to distinguish colors. The one maintained that he could discern shades which the other could not possibly perceive, and the other as stoutly maintained the contrary. When the dispute had become quite serious, and threatened to disturb their harmony, the Slaveholder taking his friend among the cabins of his negroes, in order to convince him by a decisive test of his inferior capacity, pointed out a slave, and asked him how much white, and how much black blood there was in his composition. And the Doughface examining him, said that he thought the two colors were mixed in nearly equal quantities. Then the Slaveholder pointing to a second, a third, and a fourth, the Doughface declared that in the second the two bloods were, as in the first case, equally mixed; but that in the third and fourth slaves, there was nothing but white blood. Upon this the Slaveholder laughing, said: You Doughfaces are poor judges of color. As to the first slave, you guessed rightly; but as to the second, third and fourth, you grandly erred. For the second has but a fourth part black blood in her composition; the third, but an eighth; and the fourth, but one-sixteenth part.

I should really have taken them for pure white girls, said the Doughface.

Very true, said the Slaveholder; and your mistake comes from not understanding the art of mixing colors, and from your incapacity to appreciate the diversities of shades. No Slaveholder would have made such a mistake as you did.

In the first place we have pure whites as slaves, and the study of the habits and complexion of these pure whites, helps greatly to the discerning of the mixed colors. We are not at all partial as to color in extending the benefits of Slavery. We would as soon have whites for slaves as blacks; and you will accordingly find among us many in which it would be difficult even for a Slaveholder to distinguish the black blood. Then we make it a point to multiply the mixed colors with the greatest possible rapidity, and in this way we learn very much in the art of distinguishing them. You Doughfaces have a great horror of this practice, but we who are the chivalrous sons of the South, know nothing of such a horror. Look over our plantations, and learn a lesson. Do you not perceive what a variety of colors exists upon them? We all study in the school of Titian, even before we attain our full manhood. We are fond of colors. For our mixed varieties of slaves bring the highest prices. How then should we not do all in our power to augment the varieties? We do exert ourselves to this end. Do you wonder, then, that we are artists, skilled in chromatics?

Now it gives us much amusement to witness the horror of Amalgamation which prevails in the North. We think you have no taste for the fine arts. When you cry Amalgamation, we turn with immense satisfaction to our negro cabins, and fall to contemplating the colors. Here, say we, in the practice of the fine arts, is one grand reason of the wonderful superiority of the North to the South. Look at the genius of the South! Behold her skill! her parti-colored creations! these trophies of the triumphs of gifted artists! Hue blended with hue! shade melting into shade! black converted through yellow, by imperceptible gradations, into the purest white!

Why, said the Doughface, in the North, we are terrified at the bare thought of such combinations.

We are well aware of that, said the Slaveholder. But you perceive the South rather like Amalgamation; first, for the sake of the colors, and then because the parti-colored bring so good a price. Of course, we delight to have you make a great uproar about the danger of Amalgamation; for while you Doughfaces are dilligently terrifying the People, lest through the spread of freedom it should become general, we, the chivalry, are both practising it, and reaping the fruits of it in money. The tide of Amalgamation is now at its height, and as long as you will spread the belief that the freedom of the slave will increase it, so long shall we keep it at its height. For emancipation would decrease the practice amazingly, as every Slaveholder knows.

Then said the Doughface: Does Amalgamation go on more rapidly because Slavery exists?

Of course, said the other. And because the Slaveholder is the only *voluntary* party to it.

If it is voluntary only on one side, said the Doughface, there seems to be no very great harm in the practice, and it might as well become general on that condition, as be limited to you Slaveholders.

There you touch us in a tender spot, said the Slaveholder. We prefer to have a monopoly of the business. We govern the Union, we make the Presidents, we officer the Army and Navy, we are first in all the concerns of the nation; should we not be first in Amalgamation?

Certainly, said the Doughface. But are there none in the North whom you would admit to be sharers in this peculiar privilege?

None, said the Slaveholder, but those who make the greatest outcry against it. For those are the very fellows who strengthen our monopoly.

Then the Doughface, feeling that he had learned the way to distinction, bade adieu to his friend, and from that day forward never ceased to declaim on the danger of Amalgamation.

XLVIII.

THE PROSPECTS OF THE WOULD-BE CANDIDATES.

Whoever would be a Democratic President should not be an open advocate of Universal Liberty, neither should he do too much, or too little, for Slavery.

SEVERAL northern Doughfaces who were desirous to know their prospects for a nomination to the Presidency, went together to consult a Slaveholder in regard to the matter, having resolved to make a brief statement of their merits, and request his opinion. The Slaveholder received them very condescendingly, and agreed to give them his views of their respective prospects, if they would each tell as much of the truth about their political deserts as they could bear to utter.

Then the first began and said: The conditions on which you are to express your opinions, are rather hard for me to accept. I have never been in the habit of speaking the truth in political matters, and this very confession is as frank an avowal as I have ever made. I have sought office ever since I came to adult years, and I have been tolerably successful thus far. I have *professed* Democracy, and that is all; I never had any faith in it except as a highway to preferment. In fact, I was in early life a federalist. I have been a candidate for the Presidency once, and intend to send in my name to the nominating convention, every four years, as long as life lasts. I have been a foreign minister, and once had the honor of indirectly preventing the overthrow of the slave-trade. I have received large sums of money from the federal government, and considerable glory that I did not deserve. I have been a member of the Senate for a long time, and shall hang to that place as long as I breathe, unless I am elected President. I wrote a letter into the South which conceded the principle that the Slaveholder has a natural and constitutional right to plant Slavery wherever there is an inch of free soil. I showed the North that the only way to extinguish Slavery is to diffuse it, and the northern Democracy believe it to this day, though I never did. It is worth something to establish so grand a lie in the faith of a whole people. But if, as a southern statesman has said, an overflowing treasury is a great danger to the nation, I may perhaps say that my principal merit has been in resisting with all my might the progress of that danger. For I have either been quartered on the treasury myself, or had some relative fastened upon it, for forty years.

Then the Slaveholder said: The last merit you mention ought at any time to entitle you to the Presidency. The South, by which I mean Slaveholders, always favor those Presidents who know how to tap the treasury. We by no means put the money into it, but we do take it out. And our great difficulty has been to get it out in apparently legal ways, as fast as the People put it in. All the wars we Slaveholders originate, and all the fictitious claims we compel Congress to pay, do not begin to deplete it as rapidly as we could wish. But a swarm of such men as you, helps on wonderfully—not only empties the treasury, but empties it southward. This faculty of depleting public treasuries is a great merit, but in truth, the others are a little stale. The letter you mention was a great thing in its day; so was the principle of diffusing Slavery in order to extinguish it. But in these days, when we can find men mean enough to cheat the People of whole territories in the name of Popular Sovereignty, these merits seem slight. On the whole, I think your chances for a nomination rather poor.

Then the second Doughface said: I have but one merit, and that is a steady devotion to the interests of Slavery. I was never very distinguished in my political life. My natural insignificance would have kept me forever in obscurity, had not the acuteness of the South discovered my fitness for its own purposes, and raised me very suddenly to my present greatness. Now that I have tasted the sweets of a conspicuous office, it is to be expected that I should desire to hold to it. My zeal for the South is apparent to the whole nation. Can I not be a candidate?

The Slaveholder answered: The South would like nothing better than to use you still longer; but, unfortunately, we cannot give one who has been very zealous for Slavery a second presidential term. Your zeal has made you unpopular in the North, and our rule is, never to nominate one for President who is not devoted to Slavery, nor, on the other hand, one who has done so much for us as to be odious at home. Your case seems to me doubtful, though your merits are very great. Your natural insignificance makes you a valuable tool, one which it is hard to lose, but I think you must be content to sink into that obscurity from which you so suddenly emerged. I would recommend to you to submit to your fate gracefully, if you are not nominated, and devote the remainder of your life to pious exercises. The utter oblivion which is likely to overtake you, even while you live, will leave you abundant opportunity for religious contemplations, and you have a good basis for the works of repentance.

Now a third stepped forward, and said: I began life an abolitionist, and I had, when young, some conscience. But as I aspired to political distinction I abandoned my hostility to Slavery, and bid adieu to conscience, that I might have no embarrassments in the pursuits of office. And you cannot conceive how easily one rises in the political world when all sense of duty has died out of him, unless you have tried it yourself. Soon after commencing my career as a politician, I married a plantation in the South, and I now think my moral sense effectually seared. It seems to me that the trump of judgment were unable to raise in it a single twinge.

It was this desirable state of mind that prepared me to draft that law by which the People were cheated of their Great Territory. You must admit that the Slave Power has had no servant so pliant as I, none so ready to take in hand the execution of its giant iniquities, none capable of doing the People so much mischief in the name of Democracy. I have laid your whole class under eternal obligations to me.

The Slaveholder replied: In our efforts to subdue the People, and crush out their liberties, be assured that we consider you of all others the man for the Presidency. That you have no conscience, we consider one of the first qualifications for that office. Your southern plantation is a sure guaranty to us that you never will have one. Such a man we need, for we have yet a great many insults and injuries to inflict on the North. But, as is the case of your friend who has just spoken, your zeal has been too decidedly displayed. You have lost popularity in the North; and we must choose a candidate for President who, while fragrant with the odor of Democracy and Slavery combined, shall not be suspected at home of being our tool. You see our position. However, your chance for a nomination is tolerably good, for you take to our dirty work as if you were born to it, and in despicable meanness you have no equal.

Then a fourth said: I have been all my life a trimmer. In my political action I have so managed as neither to arouse the suspicions of the North, nor offend the Slaveholders. Secretly I have been in favor of Slavery, and my senatorial votes have always been cast in a quiet way for that interest. I stand tolerably fair to succeed, if nominated. The People think me on their side, and the South *know* me to be on theirs. If elected, I will go down as low in obedience to the South as any of my predecessors. My chief merit is, that hitherto I have occupied no decided public position on the Slavery question, but am ready for any meanness required of me.

The Slaveholder answered: I consider your chance better than that of either of your fellows. You have neither done too much nor too little for Slavery. You are no lover of universal liberty, and have, I suspect, very little conscience. I may say with certainty, that our nominee will be a person possessing precisely your qualifications. However, your fellows here need not be discouraged. As we Slaveholders hold the keys of the treasury, we shall endeavor to find ways and means to compensate them for any sacrifices in our cause; and they may rest assured that whenever the People are to be robbed, they shall be invited to share in the operation.

XLIX.

THE PRESIDENT ELECT.

Slavery makes Presidents of such very small Men, that most of them are amazed at their own success.

THE national election for President had passed, and from all quarters of the Union the news of the result was borne with lightning speed to the successful candidate. But he, exceedingly elated at his good fortune, late at night retired to rest. His sleep, however, was very much disturbed; for the sudden advent of great good fortune, as well as of great calamities, is unfavorable to repose. So toward the morning after election, the President started suddenly from sleep, and sat bolt upright in his bed. Then rolling his eyes and looking about him, he began to consider what had happened; and finally recovering his consciousness he began to recollect that he had gained the victory in the presidential contest. But wishing to be certain of the fact, and to know whether he was not dreaming, he shook his faithful consort who lay by his side, and waked her also. Then turning to her, he asked: Am I not elected President?

Certainly, said she, why do you ask? Do you not recollect that the telegraph brought, last evening, the returns from more than half the states?

I do now recollect it, said the President; but it seemed so strange that I could not at first believe but that I had been dreaming. But now that I am conscious of being really elected, I feel rejoiced that the verdict of the People has, as it were, declared me a man of extraordinary abilities and devoted patriotism. I feel a little delicacy in asking the question, but do you not think, wife, that my intellectual and moral greatness has been the cause of my nomination and election?

Then the wife, looking up from her pillow, smiling, said: Do not examine, my dear, too narrowly into the causes of your election. You are a very good sort of a man as the world goes, and a very decent husband, but I never considered you any thing extraordinary.

The husband replied with surprise: Was it not my abilities that secured my nomination?

The wife, suppressing a quiet laugh, answered: Have you so soon forgotten that you told me you had pledged yourself to certain gentlemen of the South, that if elected you would, like a good Democrat, exert all the powers of the government to support and maintain the institution of Slavery, and make it national? I think it was this promise of yours that secured your nomination.

But did not the abilities have something to do with it? said the President.

I think not, said the wife, laughing aloud. It

was your promise, and the belief of the southern lords that you would keep it, that secured the nomination, and the election. As for the People, they never know what they are about when they elect a President. They choose as the party leaders direct, and the leaders direct as the Slaveholders command. It was your promise, my dear, that made you President. If you thought otherwise you were indeed dreaming.

So saying, she turned her face to the wall, and after another laugh fell asleep. But the President, sinking back on his pillow, turned on his side and looked long and frowningly into a mirror opposite, when he too fell asleep, with these words on his lips: Perhaps she is right; but at any rate, I am President.

Now when his administration was ended, it became apparent even to many who had aided in his elevation to office, that the wife was right—that neither his abilities nor patriotism, could have procured either his nomination or election.

L.

THE POLYGAMOUS STATE.

Polygamy should not exclude a People from admission to the Union, when half the States practise it.

A SECT arose in the American Union from among the simple-hearted common people, which under the guidance of what they supposed to be an infallible book, grew into a great religious community, conforming to a multitude of foolish rites and evil practices which their Book and Prophet enjoined. For these simple people did not know that if God were to give infallible and authoritative revelations, they could not be given to a *few for all*, and therefore they were disposed to receive any pretended prophet who wrought wonders, as master and king. They were ignorant that God authenticates His presence by the gradual disclosure of *universal truths*, rather than by startling displays of unaccountable marvels. Thinking that God revealed himself in the greatest possible wonders, astounding miracles performed made them surrender their minds and bodies to a religious pretender, who bound them fast under a load of monstrously unnatural duties. Thus they were led by his direction and that of his successors, far into the wilderness of America in search of a Promised Land. The land, indeed, they found, flowing with milk and honey; but they made the milk and honey bitter with the gall of abominable religious usages. Among these, was the practice of Polygamy, which they adopted and justified on the authority and example of their prophets.

When now they had grown to be a great community, they applied for admission to the Union as a state. But when their application was heard before the Congress, a deputy from the free states opposed their admission, speaking in this wise:

This is an application which should not be heard for a moment. The mere mention of connecting a polygamous state with the Union, is a disgrace to the nation, and the hearing of the petition is a greater; but the actual admission would be an eternal monument of infamy. If a sense of our own dignity is not sufficient to make us repudiate connection with a community so leprous, a regard to the obligations of common decency, and to the bare profession of Christianity should impel us to it. Are we a Christian nation, and shall Monogamy prevail in one section of our Union, and a heathenish Polygamy in another? Shall the brothers and sisters of American parents neither be able to know each other, nor their own fathers? Shall incest be legalized, and fornication and adultery become national institutions? We should pause long before we bring upon ourselves this deluge of abominations.

Then arose one of the American Nobility and replied:

It may perhaps allay the sensitiveness of my friend in regard to the admission to the Union of a polygamous state, if I bring to his notice a few facts touching the quality of the Union as it now is, and also show him that there is high authority in favor of Polygamy as an institution.

This is already a polygamous Republic. It is well known, that we who constitute the American Nobility derive our proud pre-eminence over the non-slaveholding commonalty from the absolute ownership of over three millions of slaves, and from a large monopoly of the soil. Though we are but an insignificant fraction of the entire population, while we govern the *whole* people, officer the Army and Navy, make the Presidents, assume all the foreign embassies of consequence, fill the national Judiciary, and thus ray down distinction upon the common people like so many full moons, we never forget that the backs of our negroes, and the monopoly of the land, are the basis of this grandeur. If the nation has any glory, it is because we radiate it, having first absorbed it from those shining backs. My honorable friend should reflect on these things. Those slaves not only support us the Nobility, save us from the disgrace of manual labor, and sweeten our tea and coffee, but they put all the gloss on our national liberty-cap. Now they could not accomplish this, if they were tied up by monogamic marriage. A patriarchal looseness among them in this particular, we find to be not only beneficial, but to contribute indirectly an indescribable lustre to the national dignity. If our dignity, then, grows out of Polygamy actually existing as one of the domestic pillars of the Republic, how can we be disgraced, or contaminated by admitting to the Union a state in which the People at large practise it? It is only the union of like with like.

So then Polygamy does actually exist among us; and not only Polygamy, but Concubinage likewise. The slaves practise the first virtue; their masters shine in the other.

And as to the immorality of the thing, let me inquire whether all the great principles of morality are not defined in the Decalogue, by the prohibition of their opposites? If so, is Polygamy prohibited, or Monogamy ordained? Are not rather both Slavery and Polygamy connived at as existing institutions in the prohibition concerning covetousness? It seems to me we should not attempt to be wiser than Scripture, nor more righteous than the Patriarchs: especially when Christianity itself does not positively forbid Slavery or Polygamy, nor enjoin their contraries.

But if you think Christianity prohibits these institutions, we, the Nobility, will suffer you to cling to austerities which you think Christian, if you will suffer us to temper our practices with the moralities of the Old Testament, and regale ourselves with privileges permitted to Abraham, Isaac, and Jacob. We, surely, who are the keepers of the national honor, ought not to be tied down to morals in which our most remarkable natural gifts could have no proper field for development.

There is an additional reason why this polygamous state should be admitted. If it enters the Union, it *must* come in as a slave state. And, if it enters as a slave state, will not Polygamy come of itself with the Slavery? Why then trouble yourselves about the Polygamy, when you let in that to which Polygamy necessarily attaches? No one in this honorable body will object to the Slavery, because that is, as it were, the very cream of Democracy. A true Democrat, then, cannot object that his country appear among the nations adorned with one of the hitherto undiscovered patriarchal graces. As well might a peacock strut about with a single tail-feather, thinking itself arrayed in a full suit of caudal splendors, as a Democrat go boasting of a national glory with no Polygamy nor Slavery attached.

Here the Slaveholder sat down, amid the tumult of a universal congratulation, and the polygamous state was admitted without delay.

LI.

THE MUTTERING THUNDER.

The fear of Northern Bayonets keeps the Southern Slave in subjection.

A SLAVE in Louisiana said to his fellow: We outnumber the whites ten to one on these great plantations. Why do we submit to their oppression? Surely if we combine together, we should be irresistible. A few days only of united action would suffice for us to sweep our masters and their families from the face of the earth. How long shall we groan beneath the burdens which they heap upon us? How long shall the ground we cultivate be moistened with our sweat and blood? How long shall scourges mangle our flesh? Shall the sweets we extract from the cane be wasted on our indolent and cruel masters, while we wear out our lives to produce them? Shall the sun shine, and the earth bring forth her good things only for wretches who fatten on the unpaid toil of others? Shall these accursed idlers torture us forever, and make our lives worse than those of brutes. Shall they seal up the fountains of knowledge, and condemn us to eternal ignorance, only to use our strength for their own enjoyment? Let us unite against them, set fire to their dwellings, desolate their plantations, and slaughter themselves. We can do it. We are many; they are few. Indolence and luxury have made them unmanly. The physical force is with us.

Then his fellow replied: You know not our condition. True it is, that our masters are few, and that if we were to rise against them, we might soon exterminate the whole brood. But they have other slaves beside us who cultivate their grounds. The sway of our masters is greater than you imagine. Many years since, their fathers made a compact of union with the non-slaveholding whites of the North for the purpose of establishing liberty and justice, and building up a great nation. The northern whites supposed that the liberty they were about to secure, was that of all men; but our masters understood that it was the liberty of oppressing us blacks, and the whites, if possible. So after the compact was sealed, and a government formed, our masters took it under their management. And they have got the northern whites, by a sixty year's use of the government, so thoroughly possessed of the notion of their immense power and consequence, and their *rights* as slaveholders, that they think our masters gods. And gods they are to those base whites. For they have but to threaten disunion, and the whole crowd of them cower and tremble, like a flock of turkies at the rattling of a bladder of peas. They would no more dare to emancipate us, than to stand over a powder-magazine and explode it. Our masters have proceeded very cunningly with these timid sheep. They control their army and navy, keep up an expensive government, and make them pay the expense; and year by year they have been taking us slaves into the unoccupied territory of the Union, and spreading us about like locusts, so as to stop the increase of the non-slaveholding whites. For the whites cannot multiply if we occupy all the ground as slaves, and do the freeman's labor for nothing. All the while our masters keep up a great hue and cry about their rights—meaning their rights to our persons and labor. And they have really brought the northern whites to stand so much in fear of violating their pretended rights to our real ones of life and liberty, that, as I said before, they have no more courage than we, to rise and emancipate themselves and us. A single act of Congress would raise us to the dignity of men, save their nation from despotism, and their descendants from unheard-of depths of degradation. But those miserable northern whites stand in such terror of our masters, have such an insane reverence for their devilish compact of union, and are so bewildered among legal and constitutional mole-hills, which they consider mountains, that they have no courage for such an act of Congress. They dare not extinguish the power of our masters at a single blow. The northern *millions* are cowards before the southern *thousands*. Are they not then slaves as well as we? slaves a little higher in rank, with a little longer chain, daily shortening? They have courage only to aid in keeping us in bondage. If we were to raise the standard of freedom, they would rush in crowds to subdue us. Their bayonets support our master's liberty, and ours and their own slavery. We must wait till the vices of our oppressors have diminished their numbers, and multiplied ours many fold, till the northern whites grow sick of their union, and then will we strike! In one generation more, our children will bring the sons and daughters of our masters to judgment!

LII.

THE SURE SAFEGUARD.

The Slaveholder relies on the North as a last resort for protection against the insurrection of his Slaves.

A TEXAN planter was visited by a guest from Europe, who wished to study into the sources of the prosperity of the Great Republic. We have heard beyond the ocean, said the guest, of the wealth, domestic comfort and peace of American citizens, and I have come hither to see for myself on what basis your superiority in these respects, to us of the old world, rests. For if you have made a discovery of new principles of social order by which the citizens of civilized states may secure liberty and happiness, I desire to promulgate them.

Then said the planter: You did well to come hither to make a study of the principles of true liberty and social security, for we in America have discovered all that the human race may ever presume to know touching these matters. As domestic institutions are the foundation of the prosperity of the state, I think I can show you a model worthy of universal adoption.

So he took his guest into a field of sugar-cane where five hundred men and women nearly naked, were toiling together, and several overseers, with stout lashes, were encouraging them with brutal cruelties.

There, said the planter, pointing to the wretched bondmen, there is *one* source of American prosperity and glory, and one example of American liberty. The creatures whom you see before you are the producers of a large share of our happiness. Out of their toil and sweat comes our enjoyment, our peace, our plenty. You have there, in miniature, the social order which is the essence of American glory, and the true exemplar at which all civil institutions should aim. Society should be divided into two classes, one to enjoy, and the other to produce the means of enjoyment. The enjoying class should rule the producers, and they should be divided again into two classes—the first owned by the enjoyers, and the second controlled by them, but allowed to vote. There should be a distinction of colors between the producers also. The producers which are owned directly by the masters, should be black; and those which are controlled by their masters without knowing how it is done, should be white. The masters should be as white as circumstances will permit. I need not inform you that we masters, or Slaveholders, for this is the better name, own nearly four millions of blacks, and govern about twenty millions of the other color. We have a kind of compact with our white servants by which we govern them. The chief articles of the compact are, that we shall give them presidents, foreign ministers, judges, generals, and navy officers whenever they are needed, on condition that they shall support them. This compact adds largely to our enjoyment. We are the Nation—we are America. When the constitution of European society is divided into these three classes, the slaveholders, slaves, and semi-slaves, you will begin to have a permanent social order. But you are sadly in want of a black basis.

There is a short process by which you can get an equivalent, which I will briefly indicate. You have a nobility in Europe who have lost their serfs in the revolutions of ages. Let this nobility in each country select out a pretty large percentage of the producing class, and allow them to vote under a constitution, on condition that they shall always elect members from the nobility to be presidents, judges, and so forth, pay them good salaries, and hold their brother producers in slavery. In order to keep this body-guard of the nobility in obedience, let it have a Congress, and give the Congress annually a batch of laws to enact which will more and more curtail their own liberties. This business of law-making is very congenial to the human heart, and if you of the nobility initiate all the laws, and spice them occasionally with flagrant inhumanities, you will always keep your body-guard up to their duty. As names are more powerful than things, with the unthinking crowd, let your toiling, self-enslaving voters be called THE DEMOCRACY, and the system will work to a charm.

After *The Democracy* have gone on voting a short time, make them *vote away the right of voting itself;* then you will have but two classes in society—slaveholders and slaves. There is where we intend to bring up in America.

Your plan, said the guest, seems very feasible, and would command, I should think, general attention throughout Europe. It is worthy of profound consideration. I should fear, however, occasional terrible insurrections, where society is divided into but two classes—slaveholders and slaves. How would you propose to obviate that difficulty.

Said the planter: At the moment when a civil society resolves itself into slaveholders and slaves, you will find its national democracy spontaneously decomposing into a *standing army*, on the one hand, and a few *office-holders and hireling legislators* on the other. When national democracies collapse by their own rottenness, there is generally very little left but those three elements.

And do you anticipate such a result, said the guest.

We Slaveholders expect it, said the planter.

But how would you put down an insurrection of these strong-handed blacks, should they rise now before your standing army is fully formed?

That is all provided for by our glorious Constitution, said the planter. We have also a sure safeguard in the servile temper of our laboring white millions; particularly the northern ones. They are afraid to release their black brethren from our hands by any direct act. Whenever they show any inclination that way, we rattle the parchment of the Constitution over their heads, and they cower before us like spaniels. They have the greatest regard for what they call *our rights*, and are afraid to create at once over *three millions of free citizens*, through fear of offending a *few thousands of us petty tyrants*. So in the event of any serious insurrection on the part of our black slaves, we have but to call out our northern white ones, whose courage is sufficient to withstand the millions of their fellow-slaves, but evaporates altogether before the frown of a single Slaveholder.

If that is the temper of your northern slaves, said the guest, you are surely well defended against insurrection.

We certainly are, said the planter.

LIII.

THE CABINET COUNCIL.

The greatest perplexity of American Presidents and their Cabinets, arises from a desire to strangle the Liberty of the People.

AFTER Popular Sovereignty had been, as he thought, effectually destroyed in the Great Territory stolen from the People, there came tidings to the Chief Magistrate of the Republic that the free settlers in the territory would not submit to be governed by any but their own laws. News also came that a town of these freemen was beleaguered by slaveholders from an adjoining state, who wished to force the settlers into obedience to a slave-holding code. When the Magistrate heard of these things he was very much perplexed; for he wished to appear to the People to be a supporter of Popular Sovereignty, but he desired to be in reality the maintainer and defender of the sovereignty of Slaveholders. So he called a cabinet council to deliberate on the proper course to pursue in so grave an emergency, for the invading Slaveholders were clamoring for a band of national soldiers to subdue the freemen to obedience to the laws ordained for them.

Now when the cabinet council had assembled, the Master of the Forces, who was fiercely desirous that the invading Slaveholders should be seconded, spoke to the Magistrate in this wise: This is an emergency in which your respect and zeal for our order, and your sense of gratitude for the honor conferred on you by making you President, can be most signally displayed. Recollect, sire, that you were elected for the express purpose of defeating and destroying Popular Sovereignty. We admit that thus far your management has been most adroit. Even Slaveholders did not imagine you to be capable of such sublime impudence as to attempt to destroy the freedom of the People under the very name of that freedom. You have begun well; you only need to follow up your past acts with an audacity equal to that you have already exhibited. Your messages and proclamations are everything a Slaveholder can desire. No man living can say one thing and mean another better than you. No one can better amuse the People with false promises; and your democracy is unexceptionable. But all these closet faculties are nothing, unless followed up by decisive practical measures. Order out the national soldiery to aid the Slaveholders in repressing popular freedom in the new territory, and your work is done. But if you hesitate, remember that there are plenty of doughfaces still remaining, from among whom presidents can be made, and that he who is most subservient to us, is most likely to occupy your place.

Then the Magistrate replied: I am surrounded

with difficulties on every hand. Whichever way I turn, some grave and overwhelming obstacle seems to obstruct my progress. I love office, I love money, I love praise. These are the great objects of my existence. When in the pursuit of them, I can do a turn for conscience, I sometimes perform a duty; though this is seldom; I naturally wish to appear well before the People, and I am equally anxious to secure the approbation of the Slaveholders who rule the People. Office and money come from you, praise from the People. I am now in a crisis in which office, money, and praise seem to be put in jeopardy. It will not do to call out the national soldiery, for that will bring matters to a pass in which it will be necessary to throw off all disguise in the matter of Popular Sovereignty, and disclose my real sentiments. Neither will it do to withhold the soldiers, for then the Slaveholders will lose the control of the territory. The subject fills me with the intensest anxiety; my sleep is disturbed; my digestion is irregular; my democracy has struck in—

Here the Magistrate changed color, and before his associates were aware, had fainted in his seat. Gathering around him, one suggested one remedy, and another another, to restore him; but the Master of the Forces putting them all away, advanced, and making a few mesmeric passes over his head, whispered these words: *You shall be the next nominee,*—when to the surprise of all, he slowly opened his eyes, and sitting a few moments, apparently recovered his full consciousness, when he arose and left the room.

Then said the President's Lawyer: Our next democratic President must be a man of more nerve, if the government is to be administered with efficiency and dignity. These fainting fits derange everything.

It would be just as well, in my opinion, said the Master of the Forces, if the next democratic President were to have no will at all; for then some of his Cabinet could act and speak for him on all occasions. The difficulty with this one is, that sometimes he has no will of his own—when we counsel for him; and then he recovers resolution, and goes so fanatically to work, that he knocks all our plans into pieces, which makes the doings of our administration bear a very checkered look. These fitful, fainting Presidents are not the thing.

Well, said the Lawyer, in the present emergency, I would recommend that the United States soldiers be sent into the territory, not to repress the efforts of the Non-Slaveholders openly, but ostensibly to keep order. Meantime their officers can lead on the border Slaveholders to thwart every effort for freedom on the part of the free state settlers. Thus while we are apparently keeping order, we can thoroughly establish Slavery.

When this plan was proposed, it met the approbation of the Cabinet, and the national soldiery went forthwith to the new Territory to keep order; and the order which they kept was such as rules in Warsaw.

LIV.

THE INSURRECTION.

Resistance to Tyrants is obedience to God.

A SOUTHERN orator pronouncing an oration on the national holiday, said: There are two maxims which the freeman should ever remember and practise. One is, that eternal vigilance is the price of liberty. The reason of this is found in the constitution of man and society. The love of power and property will always be the two passions which will most strongly engross the human breast. The love of power makes the possessor of that passion capable of commanding, and commanding with severity, and a genius for command extorts an involuntary deference from the masses of men, and that deference is followed by obedience. The natural ruler of men is acknowledged by a species of magnetism wherever he makes his appearance. He orders, and there is submission; he wills, and his will is law. Such men at once organize and enslave society. In time, the one natural ruler must quarrel with his peers to maintain even a partial supremacy. Then the masses take one step toward the possession of their rights. For when equal lords fall out, they must buy the aid of each other's vassals, by conceding privileges. But if the quarrel be long continued, then one lord at last having destroyed all his equals, rules supreme over all the vassals, by prerogative alone. Then prerogative dies, and property rules over a people equal before the law. But as property goes on accumulating in fewer hands, it deserts the People more and more, the men of power join with the men of property to establish laws to extend the area of Poverty, and finally the People return to that vassalage which was their original condition. So the maxim, *Eternal vigilance is the price of liberty*, means, *Let the people beware of a perpetually increasing inequality of property*. But if the People have become mere tenants at sufferance of the earth, if they are reduced to Poverty and Servitude, then they may well practise the second maxim: Resistance to tyrants is obedience to God. For as the tyrant rules by a sheer outrage on the rights of his slave, the forcible overthrow of the tyrant becomes the establishment of those rights which God ordains, and is, therefore, obedience to Him. This maxim is so nearly self-evident, that reasoning cannot make it clearer. The victim of the tyrant feels it to be true.

Now a number of slaves were preparing a banquet within hearing of the speaker's voice, and the words which he had uttered struck home, and one said to another: If resistance to tyrants is obedience to God, then we have a way in which we can obey God. Surely we who are robbed of all our earnings save a mere pittance of food and clothing, are poor; surely, we who are denied the pursuit of happiness, and the enjoyment of life; who cannot marry, but only live in concubinage; who can possess no property to call our own, and no certain home but the grave; who are compelled to sweat that others may enjoy; to live in daily fear of the scourge, and worship only as our taskmasters say, are slaves. Certainly they who inflict all these ills upon us, while they boast of their own freedom—they are the tyrants! and resistance to *them* is obedience to God! Let us put in practice, what our teacher recommends.

So they formed a conspiracy against their masters. And not long thereafter, there arose at midnight, over a wide district among the homes of the Slaveholders, the flames of burning houses. And the groans of strong men slain in darkness, and the wails of women and children, looking at the slaughter of husbands and fathers, were heavy on the winds, and the smoke of blood filled the heavens. For the rage of the risen slaves knew no bounds, and they were sending their masters to judgment, believing that resistance to tyrants is obedience to God.

LV.

THE NATIONAL GLORY.

National Glory consists in the possession of a Sound Democracy, a series of Democratic Presidents, and a laboring class of Slaves, governed by a corps of Slaveholders.

An Alien, dining with the Chief Magistrate of the American Union, conversation turned on the question, What constitutes national glory? and after the Alien had expressed his own opinion, he asked the Magistrate to declare his, saying, that one in his position must be expected to know what true glory is, better than persons in a private station. So that great officer, first drinking a glass of wine to clear his throat, turned to the Alien and the other guests at the table, and proceeded to speak in this wise: You did well to ask my opinion. I am acquainted with glory individually, and I know in what the glory of a nation consists. And as the result of my studies, I come to the conclusion that there are four elements in the latter. The first is, a numerous laboring population, or productive class. As a nation needs for a basis of its strength an ample supply of the necessaries of life, it needs multitudes to till the ground, to raise its grain, its cotton, its sugar, to open its mines of iron and coal, to build its cities and ships, and construct its highways. But as cotton and sugar are the greatest necessaries of life, the greater part of a nation's laborers should be made to produce these without wages, so that the nation shall get these valuable products at the least cost. The producers of all other necessaries save cotton and sugar, should be paid just as small wages as it is possible to get their work for. These two classes of laborers should lie at the foundation of the social edifice, and the edifice itself should rest, as it were, on their backs. The institution of these two classes of servile laborers is the basis of national glory.

The second element of that glory is a sound Democracy, by which I mean a People resolutely bent on keeping up the two classes of laborers by their votes,—one class as I said to labor for nothing, and the other for next to nothing. Undoubtedly such a people would be a little blind to their own interests, inasmuch as all the laborers must at last come from their ranks. But that blindness adds all the more to the glory. A People ready to vote itself into any condition at the behests of its party leaders, is peculiarly blessed.

The third element of national glory is a body of lords, or gentlemen, who shall own the producers of cotton and sugar, and be joint stock-holders of the sound Democracy. Such an order of lords, seems to me the very bright point in all the glory, a kind of *gloria in excelsis*. They would constitute a fountain of grandeur and greatness perennial and inexhaustible.

The fourth element is a series of democratic Chief Magistrates, by which I understand a body of agents of the lords, who shall execute their ordinances, and be appointed by them through the blind action of the People to empty the treasury, and keep the people in subjection to the lords.

These are the prime elements of national glory, in my view. As things are, it is hard to make the real conform to the ideal. A more perfect system would be one in which the sound Democracy should all be converted into serviles of the first class, so that the nation would be constituted after this model: Lowest stratum in society, Slaves. Second, National Officers. Third, or top-most order, Lords, or Slaveholders.

My own policy as Chief Magistrate, has always been directed towards this ideal social system. The more you can impoverish the free laborer, the more rapidly you can bring him to the condition of a slave. The shortest way to accomplish this end, is to bring the slave to work beside the freeman. He, laboring for no wages at all, soon brings the freeman to the same terms. Thoroughly impoverished, he ceases to be a landholder, his lands pass into the hands of the Lords, and his political freedom goes with it. When we have stripped our Democracy of their lands and living wages, we shall dispense with their services; at present, *we need their votes to bring them to that condition.* I think they may be safely counted on to extend Slavery into the virgin territory of the republic, and into all the so-called free states. I take inexpressible delight in seeing them forge their own fetters, and they have done more in that way during my administration than ever before.

Beside the constitutive elements of national glory, there are certain ornaments and graces that sparkle in it, which need to be mentioned.

One is, a sound Democracy, bound by law to chase the slaves who are one degree lower than themselves, and return them to their common masters. The actual operation of this law developes actions whose beauty must be seen to be felt. America has already produced a peer to the Roman Virginius, in the person of a slave mother, who slew her offspring to preserve it from violation. I feel a great delight in the reflection, that my hand is on the screw whose pressure can extort from the servile heart displays of virtue so enchanting.

Another ornament is the traffic in slaves. When this is carried on under the very folds of the national flag, there is a grace in it which no tongue but an angel's can adequately describe. Especially is this true, when young infants are sold from their mother's arms. In a scene of that kind, the last and most delicate lustre of our glory comes conspicuously to view, dazzling the eyes of all beholders.

But still another grace can be found in prohibiting the settling of new territories by persons opposed to Slavery. Where, as in this country, the People emigrate to unoccupied districts with the avowed purpose of establishing free institutions, it is a glorious exhibition to see the national soldiery employed to harass and destroy them, to burn their towns and villages, and to support Slaveholders in robbing and murdering them. In my administration, the world has witnessed for the first time scenes like these. Even Greece and Rome, when establishing colonies, did not require Slavery as a *sine qua non* in the founding of new states. It was reserved for me long after Greece and Rome had perished, to show on what basis new states should be built. I feel proud of my position and proud of the fame which shall be mine in posterity. I think no President, not excepting the immortal Washington, will stand so fair in history a hundred years hence, as myself. For the world will point to my monument, and say: There lies one who understood in what consists national glory, who knew how to temper liberty with conservative elements, and force America forward to ideal heights of felicity, by transforming the People into Democrats and slaves. This is the patriot who suppressed freedom in Kansas by the strong arm of the government, and elevated the Slave Power to undisturbed dominion over the whole People. *Requiescat in pulvere.*

Then answered the Alien: I am happy to hear so clear an elucidation of the sources of national glory, and when I return to Europe, I shall take great pleasure in unfolding these views to poor Frenchmen and Germans, and refer to the President of the great Republic as my instructor. For while they set forth a glorious model of social relations to those nations, they will afford great encouragement to all in the old world struggling for liberty, and will not offend the ruling powers.

And while you are expounding them to the enslaved masses there, I hope, said the Magistrate, you will not forget to inform them that America is the home of the oppressed of all nations.

Certainly, said the Alien, I shall not forget to mention so patent a truth.

LVI.

THE CHIEF MAGISTRATE ENTRANCED.

When a Pro-Slavery President speaks the truth, he is in an abnormal condition.

A PRESIDENT made a great *levee*, and invited all the Embassadors of the foreign powers, the Heads of Departments, the Congressmen of his party, and many citizens, to be present. So they all came, and crowded a great drawing-room of his palace, and the Magistrate took his stand to receive them. But now as he was putting forth his hand to salute the first of his guests, a strange paroxysm seized him. His limbs were violently convulsed, his eyes rolled back in his head, great drops of sweat stood on his forehead, and a paleness as of death gathered over his features. Then the crowd were frightened, thinking that a fit had come upon him, and were about to remove him from the room, when standing rigid in his place, he began to speak in these words:

There come crises in the history of all great nations, when they are tried by their evil genius. If they pass the trial wisely, they continue to prosper for indefinite periods; but if they fail, they go

THE CHIEF MAGISTRATE ENTRANCED.

on rapidly to decline, and finally cease to exist. This nation is passing one of these periods of trial. It is a question with her of Freedom or Slavery. If Freedom become national, her glory will grow brighter and brighter for ages to come; but if Slavery become national, her career will be short, and mean, and miserable. The masses, white and black, will be reduced ere long to the level of a common servitude. Great lords will arise upon the backs of slaves to absolute despotism over the People themselves. They will quarrel with one another, marshal the People in bloody factions, and lead them by a swift descent to utter ruin. The individual who is now unconsciously addressing you, is an agent of the genius of Universal Slavery. A consummate hypocrite, he would cheat the People themselves of the power of self-government, and do it in the very name of Democracy. He is servile and selfish to the last degree. For the Presidency, he would sell his country and all its rights forever, to the Slave Power. He has no conscience in these matters whatever. He despises the People, while he flatters, and he flatters to betray them. He is only one of a long list of greedy cormorants, who are using the name of Democracy to deceive the People, in order to fatten on their good things. He who now speaks to you is no worse than others who are eager for his place. He is a pliant tool of the accursed Power that rules your nation,—a tool which they are using to rivet irrevocably upon you the chains of the most contemptible despotism. May this nation learn to despise creatures who make use of Slavery to climb into power,—creatures like the speaker, who will stick at nothing that will aid in the extension of Slavery, and the destruction of liberty.

Here several of the bystanders became very much excited, and rushing in upon the Magistrate, they dragged him away to a private room. But he soon recovering, could not believe what they declared he had said of himself. For, said he, I do not even *think* the truth in these matters. How then could I speak it?

LVII.

THE UNEXPECTED PROPHECY.

The Slaveholders are not the South.

By the parlor-fire of a southern hotel, sat a party of Slaveholders conversing on the best means of keeping the People blind to their proceedings, and maintaining their control of them, when one said: The South must first of all claim the right to immigrate to any territory of the Republic with her slaves. We must represent that the exclusion of ourselves and our property from any portion of the country is a crying injustice, in conflict with the Constitution, and which if persisted in, will result in a dissolution of the Union. For we can easily make the People believe that the South has the integrity of the Union in her own keeping, and that if we once withdraw our support, the country would become a prey to anarchy, and the People would have no protection from foreign enemies. They think now that their salvation depends upon an alliance with us, and we must harp on that string till it becomes an impression so fixed that their children will be born with a constitutional fear of disunion and reverence for Slaveholders. We must teach them to inquire on all occasions when a new political measure is proposed, What will the South think of it? So that if they need a tariff on imported goods, they will ask first, Does the South wish it? If they wish a rail-road to the Pacific, they will ask, Where will the South be pleased to have it built? If they wish a President, let them inquire, Does the South like the man? Is there public money to be expended? Let them first run and see if we cannot use it for them. Is the country to be represented at foreign courts? Let them look around for a Slaveholder. The People are servile already, but not nearly so much as they should be. We must fill their stupid heads full of awe for the South, and get them unchangeably habituated to wait our orders, and do our pleasure. The South likes this, the South dislikes that—such considerations should control all their public action. And if we can get our slave institutions free admission into all parts of the Republic, then all that may come to pass in a degree of which we do not now dream. For when our Slavery is every where tolerated, we can put our feet on the necks of the People themselves. How magnificent will be the power of the South, when we own as property, not only our Slaves, but the whole body of Non-Slaveholders—when we become the government, and are enabled to restrict one by one the liberties of the People, and finally establish a monarchy! We are the South, and the People shall be our slaves, with those we already have.

Now one of the Southern People sat listening to this discourse, and being exceedingly incensed, he turned to the Slaveholders and said: You scoundrels! who made you the South? You contemptible crew of tyrants, who number in all but three hundred and fifty thousand, who constituted you the lords of the People? By what arts have you succeeded in arrogating to yourselves the government of this Union? You forsooth are the South, because you own three millions of Slaves, and keep six millions of us Non-Slaveholders in abject poverty. And you claim a right to carry Slavery wherever the Non-Slaveholder may go! Is it to keep us forever poor, that you claim it? Do you wish to own all the land of the Union, as well as all the bodies of its People, that you set up such a claim? Where shall be the People's homes, if your plantations cover all the earth? How shall the Non-Slaveholder get pay for his labor, if you compel millions to work for nothing? A right to take slaves with you into the territory of the People! No; you have no right even to *hold* a slave, much less to use him to deprive us of homes and of labor. This we are beginning to understand. We Non-Slaveholders will first shut out your slaves from the new territories of the Union, and then we will emancipate them. We will enlarge the areas of freedom from the very doors and hearth-stones of you Slaveholders. We will compel you to pay them wages, that we may find wages ourselves. We will force you to let them go and come as they please, in the pursuit of happiness, that our own liberty may be enlarged. Remember that by using the powers of Congress to extend your oppressions, you have set us the example to use the same powers, in extending liberty; and *the day is not far distant, when an act of Congress shall break every chain in the land.* Remember, that when the People move for freedom, it will be the descent of an avalanche, irresistible and overwhelming. Not long hereafter, and there will be no slaveholding embassadors to foreign courts, no slaveholding judges, no slaveholding generals, no slaveholding legislators, for the land will be purified of the whole brood of you. You shall be exterminated as Slaveholders by the fiat of the People.

LVIII.

THE PATRIOT'S PORTRAIT.

American Statesmen are expected not so much to love Liberty as to profess a love for it.

An American embassador to England, by accident discovered an original portrait of one who two centuries before had been a great benefactor to that country, by his sturdy resistance to the oppressive acts of the monarch who ruled it. Thinking to achieve some honor as a lover of liberty, and to get somewhat of the old patriot's glory reflected upon himself, the embassador procured the portrait and sent it to the American Congress, that it might be kept as a precious memorial among the nation's sacred relics. But when a motion was made in the Senate for its reception, discussion arose upon the motion, and a Slaveholder expressed his sentiments in these words:

It strikes me, honorable Senators, that we ought not to be overhasty in receiving gifts of this kind. The personage whose portrait is here offered to us so freely, if I rightly recollect, was an opponent of the constituted authorities of his people, who carried his hostility so far as actually to disobey the government, and to connive at an appeal to arms to make his disobedience effective. He professed to be devoted to the liberty of the People, it is true; but he must be poorly read in history, who is ignorant that the greatest of crimes have been perpetrated in liberty's name. I care nothing for this old patriot's professions; I look at his acts, and I find that his exertions for liberty began with opposing the powers that be. A singular commencement for displays of patriotism! a strange fountain for popular freedom, in rebellion! The king, his master, sought to extend his paternal sway farther than had been done by his ancestors, and to unite his subjects to the throne by stronger ties than they had previously felt, and this pretended patriot both kicked at the enlarged paternity, and hewed away the ties! It is clear that by honoring such a patriot we but encourage rebellion to the government, and call into life a brood of similar patriots who will find the Constitution itself none too good to be resisted and defied. For in these days when fantastic and impracticable notions of equality are rife among the People, some fanatic may soon begin to inquire how it comes that so many more Slaveholders are in Congress than a perfect equality would allow; and when he learns that we are here by a provision of the Constitution which no amendment can remove, will he not exhort the People to walk through the Constitution as if it were mere gas? So there is danger in such portraits when nationally received, on account of their suggesting notions of equality prejudicial to the Constitution.

But I feel some delicacy in receiving it, on another score. To speak the plain truth, I dislike the words *liberty* and *freedom* more than any others in our vocabulary. I am a Slaveholder, and how can it be otherwise? I never hear them without a painful inward consciousness of my relations to the Golden Rule. Of course I am not particularly fond of portraits of martyrs to liberty. It is as much as I can endure, to look every day at the flag that flies over this hall, and to listen to a President's message once a year, though the praises of liberty in this document are only stereotyped phrases, and are not supposed to mean any thing. Northern Senators, to whom the words *liberty* and *freedom* are of no especial significance, should excuse our sensitiveness to sounds, images, and pictures, suggestive of the reality for which these words stand. Because *they* are insensible to that reality, they should not think that all Slaveholders are so. I insist that it is peculiarly ungracious in them to be plying us with pictures and memorials suggestive of liberty, just because they see no particular meaning in them, and are fond of pictures and public documents.

Then a Northern Senator spoke in reply:

It appears to me, that the honorable Senator makes altogether too extravagant an estimate of the effects likely to flow from memorials of liberty. The Declaration of Independence has been publicly read in the Northern section of this Union, on the anniversary of our national holiday, during a period of eighty years, and to this day the People are not conscious of any inconsistency between professing liberty, and being governed by Slaveholders. There is no fear that pictures of English patriots distinguished for their devotion to liberty, will excite any great regard for freedom in their hearts, or make them dissatisfied with any clauses in our glorious Constitution which enable Slaveholders to rule them. And if the People do not feel any emotions of this kind, it is not expected that we their representatives should be affected by them. So that the extraordinary privileges of Slaveholders are not likely to be endangered, nor will the present Constitution cease to be their everlasting palladium.

As to the sensitiveness of the honorable Senator touching the incongruity of his professions and his practice, he ought to know that it is the first thing of which every statesman should endeavor to rid himself. To profess one thing, and practise another, is one of the great arts of statesmanship. And in America it is more in demand than in any other country. For while our People are indifferent to a statesman's practice, they do desire an indefinite quantity of talk about liberty. Only keep up the profession of regard for it, and you may *act* as you please. In general, I would say, let an American statesman's practice in regard to liberty, be in the greatest possible antagonism to his professions, and he possesses the most enduring basis for the esteem of the People, or, at least, of the sound Democracy. Do not fear, then, I would say to the honorable Senator, the influence of this English patriot's portrait. Do not be afraid to look at it on account of its suggesting any thing unpleasant touching the Golden Rule. Do not send it away to the hall of the Patent Office, nor to the National Institute, nor into the Supreme Court-room. But let us bring it into the hall of the Senate, and suspend it above the chair of the speaker, so that while we are passing Fugitive-Slave bills, destroying Popular Sovereignty, annulling old Compromises and patching new ones, we may grin defiance at the picture of the old English patriot, congratulating ourselves that while we are uprooting the liberty he struggled to establish, we are making the world ring with our professions of devotion to it.

This recommendation was heard with a murmur of delight; and the patriot's portrait was reserved to adorn the hall of the Senate, so that there might ever be in sight a souvenir to remind that honorable body of the liberty which it is so inclined to destroy.

LIX.

THE BESOTTED ALIEN.

The Alien who would ostracise the native Colored Man, should not be surprised to find himself ostracised by the native White.

A NATURALIZED citizen about to cast his first vote in America, was solicited by a National Democrat to act with his party, as no other in the country loved and defended the freedom of universal humanity. Being asked to show how this love for freedom was manifested, the Democrat said: You know, perhaps, that we have in our land a great multitude of blacks. More than three millions of them are slaves, and it is very well that they are. They have been trying for nearly a hundred years to make slaves of us white people, but they have not succeeded yet. They are a very dangerous class of society. They come into the North and seize upon all the lucrative occupations which we whites ought to have, and thus prevent our getting a comfortable living. The business of barbers, boot-blacks, hostlers, and chimney-sweeps, is nearly all monopolized by them, and they leave us nothing but agriculture, the mechanic arts, and commerce to attend to. Pretty soon we whites, you perceive, will have nothing to do. But that is not all. These blacks have a terrible hankering for Amalgamation, particularly with Democrats; and we stand in mortal fear that the time is not far distant, when we shall all lose our pure white color, and not know to which race we belong. There is but one escape for us from this impending calamity. The proprietors of the National Democracy, who reside in the South, and own already between three and four millions of blacks, are ready to meet this danger of Amalgamation half-way, and take the whole practice of it into their own keeping. But to this end they wish us to surrender all the vacant territory of the Republic to them, so that they can collect all the black population of the country into the far West, and carry the business to heights which no man can measure. They say they can make it profitable, if they only had more room to operate in; and the half of the Republic not being sufficiently large for this purpose, they propose to make a slave region of all our unoccupied territory, and even convert our free states into slave parks to save us from this imminent peril. Can any project be more benevolent, or more opportune for us? You know very well that these blacks are a detestable race, and your regard for humanity ought to be so exercised as to save the pure Democracy from contamination. Vote with us, and all will be well. Join us permanently, and you will never need to do any thinking for yourself upon any public measure.

Submit to the guidance of the proprietors of the party, and while you witness the glory of your adopted country augmenting with indescribable velocity, you will see Amalgamation vanish in unlimited diffusion.

Then said the Alien: I do not quite approve of diffusing Amalgamation to get rid of it. It seems to me that the greater the area over which you allow the negro to reside, the closer and the more frequent the contact between him and the pure democrat; and that, in time, there will be such a variety of colors involved in Slavery, that the pure white man himself will be thought none too good for it, if you allow the proprietors of the Democracy a monopoly of Amalgamation. However, I owe the detestable black race such a grudge, that out of sheer dislike to it, I will aid any party that will add new rivets to its chains.

You will then vote with us, said the Democrat.

Certainly, said the Alien.

By this course, said the other, you will experience a new pleasure—that of professing one thing, and doing another—of which if a man get but one sip, he will follow it up with so many others, that he will in time come to believe his own lies, and at last graduate a confirmed democrat.

So the Alien was numbered among the National Democracy, and cast his influence to degrade the black race. Not long thereafter, the Order of Ignorami burst into being, animated with the narrowest prejudices against aliens, and forthwith set to work to array the whole native population against them.

Then the Alien raised a great cry against oppression, and made his whole neighborhood ring with bitter declamation against the native American. And he charged that while toleration of all races and nations was professed in the land of his adoption, and a promise of free citizenship offered to the oppressed exile, that the profession and the promise were alike empty and unmeaning; that America was a home only of swaggering liars and unequalled hypocrites.

But a true friend of humanity hearing his complaints said: You miserable fool! By what right do you complain of the native white American's harsh treatment of yourself, when you cater and duck to his prejudices against the native black man? Have you so little wit as not to see that the same narrowness of soul that degrades the native negro on account of his color, is the very root of the prejudice against the alien? that he who cannot treat a black as if he were a human being, is just the one to make the accidents of birth or rank the measure of his regards for a white? Wretched dunce! how will you make the rights of the alien sacred unless you derive that sanctity from the bare quality of his human nature? With what face shall you ask for free citizenship, when you do all you can to wrest it from the native negro? Do you flee from the oppression of aristocracies of rank at home, to build up here an aristocracy of color? Do you shout democracy, and lend your aid to those who enslave millions? Then receive your reward. Suffer in silence the disgraces which our stingy-souled whites put upon you. If they disfranchise you, do not complain. Say: So would I do by the black. If they would shut you out ot all honorable employments, say: So would I do by the black. If they point their fingers at you in scorn as if you were unworthy of equality with themselves, say: So would I do by the black. Say to yourself: The injustice which I am willing to do the lowest in the scale of society, rebounds, and brings me to their level. The democracy that would enslave those whose greatest degradation is a dark skin, fosters a spirit and a party that would enslave poverty because it is helpless, and the alien because he has not native blood. I must learn so to act as to make the rights of men sacred, simply because they are men. I must cultivate no prejudices in the American people that may react against me; no prejudices against color and race, because these may by slight occasion be converted into aversion to myself. I will take care, in a world full of hypocrisies, and in a country flatulent with extravagant pretensions to freedom, to avoid being ensnared by great professions. As in my own country I always expected the greatest displays of tyranny from that quarter whence came the greatest pretensions to paternal regard for the people, so in this land, in that direction whence emanate the loudest cries for Democracy, there will I look for the most impudent and shameless disregard of it.

If you aliens would only lay such reflections to heart, and practise accordingly, you would teach our little-souled white natives some magnanimity, and fix your own rights on an enduring basis. But remember that that form of democracy that uses you to oppress the black, will itself spawn innumerable parties in time to harass you and restrict your liberties.

LX.

THE BORDER RUFFIANS.

The Border Ruffians reside in the City of the Capitol

An honest country Democrat hearing a great deal said about Border Ruffians, but not knowing what to understand by the words, called on the President of the Union, and asked what they meant, saying: These words are very mysterious to me. We democrats who live in the country, very naturally suppose that when we have made a President and the chief officers of government, we have got into one mass the concentrated wisdom and honesty of the whole nation. So we generally sit down in quiet, and trust that all things will go on very well without any further concern of ours. For we think it the part of a good democrat never to distrust our leaders, and to abide by their proceedings, as the highest possible guide of right and wrong, and to follow wherever they lead, though it should be to the place where they say the Evil One makes his home. And it is clear that if we did not follow our leaders blindly, there would be fewer democratic Presidents than there have been. But when our leaders have all the wisdom and honesty, we don't see how they can possibly get into trouble in steer ing the ship of state. For ships of state, I suppose, are not like other ships, blown along by winds from without the vessel; but the crew sit down around the sails, with large wind organs, and blow at them, in the direction they wish to go, and the voyage is made very pleasantly. How is it then in the matter of these Border Ruffians? What are they? do they embarrass the democratic administration? I hear that they give you trouble, and I don't see how it can be. Please explain who they are, and what they do.

Then answered the President: It is a very long story about these Border Ruffians, but I think I can make you understand it. There are four parties in this nation, as you may perhaps know. The Slaveholders, the Slaves, the Democracy, and the People. The second and third are almost cyphers in our political system. The first and the fourth are units. Put the democratic cypher by the slaveholding unit, and both together will attract the slave cypher to themselves, and make a hundred against the People, who are thus made a little better than a cypher. Put the democratic cypher beside the unit of the People, and they also will attract to themselves the slave cypher, and make a hundred against the Slaveholders, who will by the same process become nothing. By a democrat I understand a natural ally and tool of the Slaveholder. I am a democrat in this sense. Now the Slaveholders wish to make so many of the People democrats, that the People will become a cypher, or in other words, that they may count a thousand,

and the People nothing. Now this is the upshot of democratic policy. It may be summed up in one word: How can the Slaveholders be made everything, and the People nothing? Well, the matter stands thus: The People owned a large territory in the West, in which they were calculating to establish free institutions, such as free suffrage, free homesteads, free pursuit of happiness, equality before the law, and many other such chimeras for which a good democrat has no natural taste, and they were likely soon to occupy it, and make themselves everything and the Slaveholders nothing. Anticipating this mischief to our masters, I conceived the wittiest plan to cheat the People that ever entered democrat's head. It was to get a surrender of the whole of it to the Slaveholders, under pretence of Popular Sovereignty. The wit of the plan was, that whereas the Slaveholders had bound themselves to let the People have the exclusive right to establish the real Popular Sovereignty, I got a law passed to release the Slaveholders from their bargain, and let them into the territory, as if they were the real People. The plan was most admirable, but unfortunately some of the People saw through it, and pretending to understand my Popular Sovereignty in a literal sense, began to rush into it, and set up in the very face of the Slaveholder, those damnable free institutions I have just mentioned. I was in great perplexity. I began to fear that there would be no Slavery nor Democracy in Kansas,—nothing but Popular Sovereignty in dead earnest. But some valiant Slaveholders, at my instance, when elections were to be held for the territorial Legislature and other offices, came into the territory from an adjoining State, drove away the free settlers from the polls, voted all liberty out of the territory, and made slaveholding laws for the People there. But the laws, though of the very best ever ordained for a people, do not satisfy these free settlers. The fools are determined to govern themselves, and I have been obliged to threaten to let loose on them the army of the Union unless they submit. I am a little afraid to do this just yet; but meanwhile I urge on the border Slaveholders, to do as much mischief as they dare, and harass the settlers all they can; which they have done, and have succeeded in robbing and murdering them to a greater extent than I could have expected, under the circumstances. For they are obliged to avoid the range of a certain murderous gun which will kill a man at a distance of half a mile. The Slaveholders have courage and chivalry enough, but they act on the maxim which governed me when I was in the war: Discretion is the better part of valor. However, they have drawn upon themselves the name of Border Ruffians, by their exceeding ferocity and cruelty to the settlers. So you perceive that a Border Ruffian means one who, in the joint interests of Democracy and Slavery, is ready and willing to murder a free settler, if he can do so without injury to himself. Now as my colleagues in the government, and myself, connive at the operations of these chivalrous Slaveholders, we are the real Border Ruffians, and I wish you to consider it an honorable appellation. You should get familiar with the name as soon as you well can, and learn to prize it. In a few years, after the Democracy are called upon to establish Slavery in the free states, and to extinguish free speech and a free press, hanging and imprisoning your fellow citizens who are refractory to such democratic laws and ordinances, will become quite a common business, and in those days our masters will expect every good democrat to do his duty.

And are you and your colleagues, then, said the Democrat, the real Border Ruffians?

We are, said the Magistrate. Here in the city of the Capitol do we make our home, and here are we to be sought for.

Well, said the Democrat, may light shine on all your undertakings.

I thank you for your good intentions, said the Magistrate, but we should prefer that light would not shine on all our undertakings. It would ruin the Democracy.

Amazed at this declaration, the Democrat abruptly left his presence; for he had begun to suspect that it were better to be a mal-treated free settler in Kansas than a ruffian President at Washington.

LXI.

THE YOUNG STATESMAN.

The Cowardice of the North is the Strength of the South.

When I look at the North, said a lordling to his slaveholding father, I at times despair of our domestic institutions. Fifteen millions of freemen, masters of an immense territory which is fertile in soil, abounding in minerals, traversed by noble navigable lakes and rivers, the freemen themselves active and intelligent, strong with the aids of science and the arts,—how is it possible, I ask myself, that they should long submit to our dominion? The physical force is with them, the wealth is theirs, and there is intelligence enough among them to control these elements. How easy for them to unloose the bonds of our slave population, and add all its strength to their own. Besides, our southern non-slaveholding whites would be but too ready to join with them, if they should seriously undertake the emancipation of our slaves. I cannot understand why they submit to be ruled by us. We are but a few thousands; they count millions. How is it that they do not rise against our authority, take the control of the government into their own hands, and sweep our domestic institutions away? They profess to love liberty, and they do so far love it as to be unwilling to allow Slavery as a permanent institution in the free states. Their reluctance to obey the Fugitive Slave Law proves that. Why do they not go a step beyond submission to our dictation, and dictate a little for themselves?

There are many reasons why they do not, said the father. In relation to us, there may be said to be four classes of society in the North. There is first the lowest stratum, made up of day-laborers, hirelings, and creatures of that description, men of no property, nor intelligence, nor conscience. They are a timid and servile set, acting with no courage, excepting when on duty in a mob, and never acting in concert, except from an impulse to destroy a good thing, or to support some damnable institution which is a curse to themselves. There is next a larger class, mostly farmers, and industrious mechanics, men of property and considerable intelligence, generally moral, and as they call themselves, *law-abiding*.

The next class is that of the politicians, who live by trading and speculating in public offices. The fourth is the commercial class, who engross most of the ready means of the North, and initiate most of its laws.

Now the system of northern politics is this: The love of property is the ruling passion among the people. But property by its own laws, travels constantly from the many to the few, and there being few restrictions upon the intrinsic laws of property, the number of freeholding families is constantly decreasing, and that of its hireling and homeless day-laborers constantly augmenting. As, however, party divisions among free people must turn upon a struggle for Property, or for Power, or for both, the party divisions in the North for a whole generation have turned upon the former, and therefore the essential quarrel has been between the hirelings—the mob class—and the commercial. The first has striven, unconsciously, however, to restrict the rights of property as against man, and the other to enlarge them.

This quarrel has brought into existence the politicians, part of whom seek office from love of power and fame, but far the larger part from—*the need of bread.* These breadless and penniless politicians gather together under their banner the truly needy, and especially such *as envy the rich*, and go crusading against them in the several legislatures of the free states. But being a servile and dastardly set, they never legislate so far as to diminish the hireling class, for they need to ride into office on their backs. They are careful never to legislate so as to multiply freeholding families.

The other set of politicians who seek office from ambition mainly, take in hand the interests of bankers and merchants, in a word, of Capital, and appealing to the love of order and law, manage to combine the independent yeomanry and mechanics of the country in parties. This last set are generally unsuccessful, because they lead men who are not driven by the *spur of want*, and who will not submit to the dictation of party leaders, and who put much less value upon the triumph over an opposing party than on the triumph of a principle. The former set of politicians, on the other hand, maintain a strict party discipline, by the skill with which they inspire their followers with *the fear of being beaten*. This fear is just now the only principle of cohesion among those followers.

Political contests are, therefore, in the North, struggles to determine whether Property, as such, shall have greater privileges than Man; or in plainer terms, whether the dependent and hireling classes shall constantly augment in proportion to the independent freeholders. The dependent, or mob class, very justly say No, so far as their profound ignorance, and the devilish craft of their leaders will allow. But the commercial classes say Yes. The independent freeholders say sometimes Yes, and sometimes No, according as the issue between the competitors comes more or less clearly to light. They are in truth indifferent to the result of the contest between the two parties.

Such is the system of home politics in the North. But in the national politics, the introduction of our slave system puts these several northern parties in a different relation to each other. We of the South wish not only to make Property superior in its privileges to Man, but to convert men into property,—to make what is now a hireling class in the North, chattels personal. That is the principle of southern politics. At present we find in national politics, the hireling politicians with their mob followers, and the northern mercantile class, joined hand in hand to aid us, and the independent yeomanry of the North arrayed against us. And the reason why they do not overturn our slave system is perfectly clear, though they have the strength to do it.

The needy politicians who lead the northern mob *fear* to lose the offices, if they oppose our wishes.

The northern merchants *fear* to lose our trade.

The northern freeholders *fear* to attack Slavery because they dread to violate the Constitution.

The South may always maintain its supremacy over the North if it will only cultivate these three northern terrors.

We must thoroughly frighten the politicians with the threat of depriving them of office.

We must frighten the merchants with the threat of taking away their trade.

We must terrify the independent freeholders of the North, if they shall dream of assailing Slavery directly, by holding up to them the sanctity of the Constitution, and menacing a dissolution of the Union.

When you come upon the stage of action, my son, bear in mind these three huge bug-bears; keep them always before the North, remembering that the cowardice of the North is the strength of the South.

LXII.

THE DANGEROUS PRIVILEGE.

Colored Persons should not be allowed to testify against Whites, in cases of Church Discipline.

In a general Council of one of the American Churches, a northern delegate proposed that a certain rule of procedure in cases of discipline, in force in his Church, should be repealed. The rule forbade a colored person to testify against a white brother or sister, where such brother or sister was charged with an offense requiring trial. The delegate said: We are a Church of Christ, and as such we profess to love the Lord supremely and our brothers as ourselves. We are equals before the Lord, and we should treat each other as such, for this is an essential part of true Christianity. If a member of the Church be grieved or injured by his brother, and no atonement be made by the injurer, the aggrieved brother or sister should be allowed to bring the matter before the Church, and have it brought to a hearing. It is well known, however, that our colored brethren are not allowed this privilege, for they are not permitted to testify or complain against the white brother who may have done them a wrong. This is destroying true

Christian equality, and introducing invidious distinctions among the members of Christ's body. By taking the colored person into the Church, we act on the belief that the Lord loves him as much as us who are white. And why should he not? We shall all be of one color at the last day. We should remember what the Apostle James says: If ye fulfil the Royal Law—Thou shalt love thy neighbor as thyself—ye do well. But if ye make a difference between persons, ye commit sin, and are convicted by the law of being transgressors. By refusing our colored brethren the right of testifying in the Church against the white brother, we make a great difference between persons, and are convicted of being great transgressors. Brethren, let us stand no longer under condemnation, but let us repeal this iniquitous rule, and make the colored brother truly equal to the white before the Lord.

Then a southern delegate arose and responded:

I am surprised to see such a proposition presented to the Council for adoption. It is pregnant with mischief to the Church and to the nation. The brother who offers this resolution must be ignorant of the constitution of society and the Church in the South, or he never would have urged it. Our social system is not based on the precepts of James, neither is our Church. The whole edifice of southern society rests on a distinction of persons, a very broad distinction of persons, for a small part of the whites own the larger part of the blacks. Being property, they are treated as property, and being animated, the blacks are considered by us as beasts of burden, as cattle. This institution exists among the world's people, and we take the world as we find it. In order to introduce the Gospel, we accomodate its precepts to the world. We do not in the South wage war on sins that have grown into institutions, but we work about so as to let some roots of these sinful institutions strike into the soil of the Church; then as the institutions grow up, something of the Church's sanctity entering the sap, penetrates every twig and bough, and leaf. That is the way we consecrate human bondage. In itself somewhat wrong, we adopt it into the Church, and it is there sanctified. Thus the slave enters the southern Church in a twofold capacity, as a Beast, and as a Person, and receives a twofold treatment of course. As a Person, he is baptized, receives the sacrament, and has the Gospel preached to him; as a Beast he is scourged more or less severely, according as the demands of the cotton-field require, poorly fed and clad, bought and sold, and allowed to gender offspring for the market in a kind of quasi marriage. Now as our slaves are mostly black, does not the brother see, that if colored persons were allowed to complain and testify against their white brethren in the Church, the beastly relations of a large part of its members must necessarily cease? And if they cease in the Church will not they also be in danger of ceasing in the world? The whole social edifice would be shaken by the repeal of this wholesome rule.

But we apprehend greater danger than would result to society, within the Church itself, from its repeal. The colored females in the Church would be induced to bring charges against their masters, both clerical and lay, which, if investigated by this rule, would too often, I fear, prove true. We are extremely sensitive on this point. We of the clerical order, in particular, feel deeply. We have a reputation for sanctity which it is necessary to keep up, and the virtue of continence, alas, is nowhere strong among us. The warm climate, our sedentary habits, the example of distinguished planters in our several parishes, the high price ot comely mulattoes, and the unprotected condition of colored women, altogether form a combination of temptations, against which the rarest purity might in vain contend. And under the fostering influence of such stimuli, I need not say that the beastly relations of our church-members have attained an astonishing growth. Does our northern brother wish to have all the rare things committed in the southern branch of his Church rudely brought to light, and exposed to the laughter and derision of an impenitent world? Rather, would he not prefer, when our virtue is so little, that we should husband our reputation for sanctity and chastity with the greatest care? that we should let our light shine, lurid as we admit it to be, as far into the surrounding darkness as it can go? It is well for a Church to keep up the appearance of righteousness, even though it have nothing of the substance. We know the value of external sanctity in the southern Church, and we would like to keep our sepulchre white and beautiful without, however much uncleanliness there may be within. Is the desire unreasonable in us, situated as we are?

Let the brother imagine himself in our place. Suppose he were a pastor of a southern Church, that he had a reputation for learning, eloquence, and piety, that he were popular among the surrounding planters, perhaps the expected spouse of the heiress of a hundred negroes, a model to the country round of purity and grace. As time passes on, all the qualities for which he is admired take on a brighter lustre, and he reposes in an elysium of mingled popularity and pretended sanctity, from which he fondly dreams he is never to be disturbed. On a sudden some dozen colored women of his Church unite to charge him with a crime which I need not name, and under this rule testify against him. The charge is proved beyond all question, and in a day, as it were, popularity and pretended sanctity vanish, and the expected heiress is lost forever! This is a mere fancy sketch, it is true, but facts quite like it would too often occur, if this rule were once rescinded. I beseech our northern brethren to do as they would be done by, and let it stand.

By this eloquent appeal, the hearts of the northern brethren were profoundly affected, and recognising the severity of the necessity which lay upon their southren brethren, of protecting society and the Church against the jeers of the impenitent, and of keeping at least the outside of the platter bright and clean, they unanimously agreed to suffer the rule to stand.

LXIII.

THE INWARD MESSAGE.

The Messages of our Democratic Presidents have an esoteric sense when they treat of Slavery.

A PRESIDENT of the Union, having sent in a message to Congress, treated at considerable length, as is the manner of Presidents, upon the subject of Slavery. And the message having been read before Congress, was published abroad among the People. Now, a citizen having received a copy of it, could not well understand the sense of that portion which treated of Slavery. So he forthwith posted to the President's house, and being admitted to an audience with that officer, requested him to explain the meaning of it.

Then the Chief Magistrate, handing him a manuscript, said: In order to govern the People cunningly, all democratic officers should say one thing and mean another. For the strings by which the People are led are hidden from their sight, neither are they often exposed, nor should they be. The great art of governing them lies in the art of making pretences which are never realized. Thus, in all public documents there should be a great show of devotion to their welfare, while one really means something else. This is particularly necessary in our country, where there is a secret struggle going on for mastery between the People and the Slave Power. In all documents to be submitted to the People, it is necessary to address both these parties, but to represent the Slave Power as the aggrieved party, and to reason with the People as if they were aggressors, concealing from them the real state of matters between themselves and their opponents. In this manuscript you will find that portion of my public message which treats of Slavery, translated, or revealed in its inner sense. The inner sense we never present to the People. We Presidents experience much difficulty in so constructing our public writings as at once to blind the People and flatter the Slave Power; but I think I have succeeded as well as any of my predecessors.

So the citizen took the manuscript, and read as follows:

THE PUBLIC MESSAGE.

1. Placed in the office of Chief Magistrate as the executive agent of the whole country, bound to take care that the laws be faithfully executed, and specially enjoined by the Constitution, to give information to Congress on the state of the Union, it would be palpable neglect of duty on my part to pass over a subject like this, which beyond all things, at the present time, vitally concerns individual and public security.

INNER SENSE.—Placed in the office of Chief Magistrate as the chief tool of the Slave Power, bound to see that the functions of my office shall be as thoroughly exercised in the interests of Slavery as my capacity will admit, and specially enjoined by the Constitution to give information to Congress on the state of the Union, it would be a palpable oversight of the best means to secure a re-nomination, to let slip such an opportunity to pettifog the cause of the Slave Power, and mystify the People in a matter that vitally concerns their individual and public security.

2. It has been matter of painful regret to see States, conspicuous for services in founding this Republic, and equally sharing its advantages, disregard their constitutional obligations to it. Although conscious of their inability to heal admitted and palpable social evils of their own, and which are completely within their jurisdiction, they engage in the offensive and hopeless undertaking of reforming the domestic institutions of other States wholly beyond their control and authority. In the vain pursuit of ends, by them entirely unattainable, and which they may not legally attempt to compass, they peril the very existence of the Constitution, and all the countless benefits which it has conferred. While the People of the southern States confine their attention to their own affairs, not presuming officiously to intermeddle with the social institutions of the northern States, too many of the inhabitants of the latter are permanently organized in associations to inflict injury on the former, by wrongful acts, which would be cause of war as between foreign powers, and only fail to be such in our system, because perpetrated under cover of the Union.

INNER SENSE.—It has been a matter of painful regret to me to see States, conspicuous in founding the Republic, bearing the greater part of the expense of maintaining, while they have less than their share in the government of it, exhibit so much restlessness under the control of the Slave Power. Conscious of their ability to heal great social evils of their own, they engage in the offensive, though almost hopeless task of ameliorating the condition of the non-slaveholding whites of the South, by preventing the extension of Slavery to territories under the jurisdiction of the whole Union. In the pursuit of this end, which I fear is too easily attainable, and which it is plainly legal to endeavor to accomplish, they menace the existence of Slavery itself, and all the wonderful blessings that flow from it, as well as an amendment of the Constitution, so far as it allows Slaveholders unjust privileges in the government. While the Non-Slaveholders of the South, in the management of their own affairs, are virtually ciphers, and the Slaveholders, who are the real people in that section, very properly, in my view, aim a death-blow at the social institutions of the North by extending their own domestic institutions into the free States, too many of the People in these States are endeavoring to restrict the Slaveholders' projects, by acts which would justify the Slave Power in deserting the Union, if they had the courage to leave.

3. Is it possible to present this subject as truth and the occasion require, without noticing the

reiterated, but groundless allegation, that the South has persistently asserted claims and obtained advantages in the practical administration of the general government, to the prejudice of the North, and in which the latter has acquiesced? That is, the States which either promote or tolerate attacks on the rights of persons and of property in other States, to disguise their own injustice, pretend or imagine, and constantly aver, that they, whose constitutional rights are thus systematically assailed, are themselves the aggressors. At the present time, this imputed aggression, resting, as it does, only in the vague declamatory charges of political agitators, resolves itself into misapprehension, or misinterpretation, of the principles and facts of the political organization of the new territories of the United States.

Inner Sense.—Is it possible to present this subject as falsehood and my political ambition require, without belying the reiterated and well-founded allegation, that the Slave Power has persistently asserted claims and obtained advantages in the administration of the government, to the prejudice of the Non-Slaveholders North and South, and in which they have acquiesced? I fear not. For the allegation means that those States which have the least motive to encroach on the rights of others, to maintain their own rights, are compelled to strip off all disguise from that class whose unjust system, essentially aggressive on the rights of humanity, impels them to use the Constitution itself to extend the same injustice. In the present message, this imputed aggression may be made to appear altogether chimerical, though it is based in anything but declamatory charges of political agitators, by devising a misinterpretation of the principles and facts of the political organization of the new territories of the United States.

4. What is the voice of history? When the ordinance which provided for the government of the territory north-west of the river Ohio, and for its eventual subdivision into new States, was adopted in the Congress of the Confederation, it is not to be supposed that the question of future relative power, as between the States which retained, and those which did not retain a numerous colored population, escaped notice, or failed to be considered. And yet the concession of that vast territory to the interests and opinions of the northern States, a territory now the seat of five among the largest members of the Union, was, in a great measure, the act of the State of Virginia and of the South.

INNER SENSE.—But, if I were to speak the truth, what does the genuine voice of history say? When the ordinance which provided for the government of the territory north-west of the Ohio, and its eventual subdivision into new States, was adopted in the Congress of the Confederation, it is not to be supposed that the influence of Slavery upon such States as tolerated that institution, and of Freedom upon such as did not, escaped notice, or failed to be considered. The consecration of that vast territory to the interests of Freedom, a territory now the seat of five among the largest members of the Union, was in great measure brought about by the exertions of statesmen who loved Freedom for its own sake, and who indeed lived in Virginia, but before negroes became her great staple.

5. When Louisiana was acquired by the United States, it was an acquisition not less to the North than to the South; for while it was important to the country at the mouth of the river Mississippi to become the emporium of the country above it, so also it was even more important to the whole Union to have that emporium; and although the new province, by reason of its imperfect settlement, was mainly regarded as on the Gulf of Mexico, yet, in fact, it extended to the opposite boundaries of the United States, with far greater breadth above than below, and was in territory, as in everything else, equally at least an accession to the northern States. It is mere delusion and prejudice, therefore, to speak of Louisiana as an acquisition in the special interest of the South.

Inner Sense.—When Louisiana was acquired by the United States, it was an acquisition to the advantage of Slavery rather than Freedom, Slavery being guarantied a perpetuity by the treaty of purchase from France; for though it was a blessing to the whole country to have the region at the mouth of the Mississippi for an emporium, and though the then Louisiana was much broader in the north than in the south, extending in the north to the Rocky Mountains, we must remember that the guaranty of Slavery in one portion was virtually an abrogation of Freedom in the whole. It is mere delusion and downright lying, then, to represent the purchase of Louisiana as being as favorable to Freedom as to Slavery.

6. The patriotic and just men who participated in that act were influenced by motives far above all sectional jealousies. It was in truth the great event, which, by completing for us the possession of the valley of the Mississippi, with commercial access to the whole Confederation, attached together by indissoluble ties, the east and the west, as well as the north and the south.

Inner Sense.—The treaty stipulations guaranteeing Slavery in the act of purchase, prove that the men who participated in it, however patriotic they may have been, at least kept one eye on the interests of that institution. The purchase was, indeed, a great event, which, by completing for us the possession of the valley of the Mississippi, with commercial access to the whole Confederation, might, were it not for Slavery, be the means of binding together, in the strongest commercial ties, the east and the west, as well as the north and the south, and perhaps Canada.

7. As to Florida, that was but the transfer by Spain to the United States of territory on the east side of the river Mississippi, in exchange for large territory, which the United States transferred to Spain, on the west side of that river, as the entire diplomatic history of the transaction serves to demonstrate. Moreover, it was an acquisition demanded by the commercial interests and the security of the whole Union.

Inner Sense.—As to Florida, that was an acquisition made by an exchange of territories with Spain, and brought about by a desire on the part of the Slave Power to shut up Florida against fugitive slaves, as the entire diplomatic history of the transaction, and the millions spent in recovering fugitives from the swamps of that country, demonstrate. It was an acquisition demanded by the interests of the Slave Power, and particularly for the secure possession of their human cattle.

8. In the meantime the people of the United States had grown up to a proper consciousness of their strength, and in a brief contest with France, and in a second serious war with Great Britain, they had shaken off all which remained of undue reverence for Europe, and emerged from the atmosphere of those transatlantic influences which surrounded the infant Republic, and had begun to turn their attention to the full and systematic development of the internal resources of the Union. Among the evanescent controversies of that period, the most conspicuous was the question of regulation by Congress of the social condition of the future States to be founded in the territory of Louisiana.

Inner Sense.—But the people of the United States were growing up to a consciousness of their strength, and after suffering the Embargo Act, and wading through a war with Great Britain, evils inflicted on them by the Slave Power, to depress free labor, began to suspect the secret spring of those domestic influences which were already operative to restrict the systematic development of the internal resources of the Union. Among the controversies of that period, was one which has proved to be anything but evanescent, a question, namely, whether Freedom was really excluded from the future States to be erected out of the territory of Louisiana, by the stipulations which the Slave Power had inserted in the treaty of purchase.

9. The Ordinance for the government of the territory north-west of the river Ohio, had contained a provision, which prohibited the use of servile labor therein, subject to the condition of the extradition of fugitives from service due in any other part of the United States. Subsequently to the adoption of the Constitution, this provision ceased to remain as a law; for its operation as such was absolutely superseded by the Constitution. But the recollection of the fact excited the zeal of propagandism in some sections of the Confederation; and when a second State, that of Missouri, came to be formed in the territory of Louisiana, a proposition was made to extend to the latter territory the restriction originally applied to the country situated between the rivers Ohio and Mississippi.

Inner Sense.—The Ordinance for the government of the territory north-west of the Ohio, contained a provision prohibiting Slavery therein, subject to the condition of the extradition of fugitives from labor *due* in any other part of the United States. After the adoption of the Constitution, even if this provision had ceased to remain a law, Freedom had become so thoroughly established in the territory, that no one thought to question it by looking into the Constitution for reasons for its overthrow. But a remembrance of that provision suggested to those States in which Freedom exists, the idea of extending a similar guaranty for liberty to the whole of the unoccupied territory of the Republic; so that when a second State, that of Missouri came to be formed in the territory of Louisiana, a proposition was made to extend to that territory the restriction of Slavery originally applied to the country situated between the rivers Ohio and Mississippi.

10. Most questionable as was this proposition in all its constitutional relations, nevertheless it received the sanction of Congress, with some slight modifications of line, to save the existing rights of the intended new State. It was reluctantly acquiesced in by southern States as a sacrifice to the cause of peace and of the Union, not only of the rights stipulated by the treaty of Louisiana, but of the principle of equality among the States guarantied by the Constitution. It was received by the northern States with angry and resentful condemnation and complaint, because it did not concede all which they had exactingly demanded. Having passed through the forms of legislation, it took its place in the statute book, standing open to repeal, like any other act of doubtful constitutionality, subject to be pronounced null and void by the courts of Law, and possessing no possible efficacy to control the rights of the States which might thereafter be organized out of any part of the original territory of Louisiana. In all this, if any aggressions there were, to which portion of the Union are they justly chargeable? This controversy passed away with the occasion, nothing surviving it save the dormant letter of the statute.

Inner Sense.—Justifiable as was this proposition in all its constitutional relations, it received only the qualified sanction of Congress; the Slavery which had got already snugly ensconced in the intended new State being left undisturbed within it, while Freedom was solemnly guarantied in all territory north of a certain line. This arrangement was reluctantly submitted to by the Slave Power, as depriving it of the advantages it supposed itself to have acquired by the Louisiana treaty, and as a sacrifice of the principle that one Slaveholder is equal under the Constitution to three Non-Slaveholders. It was received by the northern States with dissatisfaction, as a concession to Slavery, dangerous to Freedom everywhere in the Union. This compromise having become a law, stood open to repeal as truly as any other act of Congress in the least favoring liberty, and was subject to annulment by the Slave Power's Supreme Court; though if Freedom were once established by it as an element of a State Constitution, its subsequent overthrow would be absolutely forestalled. In this arrangement, which principle made the better bargain, the Freedom which should exist everywhere within the Union, or the Slavery which should exist nowhere? The controversy which then arose seemed to have passed away at the time, but it has been really continued to the present day.

11. But long afterward, when, by the proposed accession of the republic of Texas, the United States were to take their next step in territorial greatness, a similar contingency occurred, and became the occasion for systematized attempts to

intervene in the domestic affairs of one section of the Union, in defiance of their rights as States, and of the stipulations of the Constitution. These attempts assumed a practical direction, in the shape of persevering endeavors by some of the representatives in both houses of Congress, to deprive the southern States of the supposed benefit of the provisions of the act authorizing the organization of the State of Missouri.

INNER SENSE.—Afterward, for example, when, by the proposed admission of Texas, the area of Slavery was to be enlarged, the controversy was renewed, and a strenuous effort was made to prevent the extension of the domestic institutions of the South, to the prejudice of the rights of the free States, by augmenting the inferiority of those States under the Constitution. Persevering efforts were made by representatives of the free States in Congress, to deprive the Slave Power of advantages which it had ingeniously pretended to find in the act which organized Slavery in Missouri, and which did not prohibit it south of the Compromise line.

12. But the good sense of the People, and the vital force of the Constitution, triumphed over sectional prejudice and the political errors of the day, and the State of Texas returned to the Union as she was, with social institutions which her people had chosen for themselves, and with express agreement, by the re-annexing act, that she should be susceptible of subdivision into a plurality of States. Whatever advantages the interests of the southern States, as such, gained by this, were far inferior in results, as they unfolded in the

progress of time, to those which sprang from previous concessions made by the South.

Inner Sense.—But the apathy of the People, and the vigorous lying of the party-leaders, finally triumphed over Justice and Liberty, and the State of Texas stole into the Union as she was, with institutions making the greater part of her people slaves, and with the express agreement by the act which appended her, that she should be susceptible of subdivision into a large number of similar slave States. If the Slave Power gained any advantages by this manœuvre, they were more than deserved, by the omission on the part of the South to prohibit Liberty in the territory north-west of the Ohio.

13. To every thoughtful friend of the Union—to the true lovers of their country—to all who longed and labored for the full success of this great experiment of republican institutions, it was cause of gratulation that such an opportunity had occurred to illustrate our advancing power on this continent, and to furnish to the world additional assurance of the strength and stability of the Constitution. Who would wish to see Florida still a European colony? Who would rejoice to hail Texas as a lone star, instead of one in the galaxy of States? Who does not appreciate the incalculable benefits of the acquisition of Louisiana? And yet narrow views and sectional purposes would inevitably have excluded them all from the Union.

Inner Sense.—To every crafty enemy of the Union—to the haters of their country—to all who long and labor for the failure of this great experiment of republican institutions, it was cause ot gratulation that such an opportunity had occurred to illustrate the advance of the Slave Power on this continent, and to furnish to the world a pledge of the weakness and instability of the Union. Who would wish to see Florida still a refuge for fugitive slaves? Who could rejoice to see Texas hugging her Slavery all alone, instead of making one in the dark girdle of our slave States? Who does not appreciate the incalculable benefits of the acquisition of Louisiana, with her Slavery intact? And yet if the destinies of the Union had not been managed mainly by Slaveholders, these territories would inevitably have been all added to it as free States.

14. But another struggle on the same point ensued, when our victorious armies returned from Mexico, and it devolved on Congress to provide for the territories acquired by the treaty of Guadalupe Hidalgo. The great relations of the subject had now become distinct and clear to the perception of the public mind, which appreciated the evils of sectional controversy upon the question of new States. In that crisis intense solicitude pervaded the nation. But the patriotic impulses of the popular heart, guided by the admonitory advice of the Father of his Country, rose superior to all the difficulties of the incorporation of a new empire into the Union. In the counsels of Congress there was manifested extreme antagonism of opinion and action between some representatives, who sought by the abusive and unconstitutional employment of the legislative powers of the government, to in-

terfere in the condition of the inchoate States, and to impose their own social theories upon the latter, and other representatives, who repelled the interposition of the general government in this respect, and maintained the self-constituting rights of the States. In truth, the thing attempted was, in form alone, action of the general government, while in reality it was the endeavor, by abuse of legislative power, to force the ideas of internal policy entertained in particular States, upon allied independent States. Once more the Constitution and the Union triumphed signally. The new territories were organized without restrictions on the disputed point, and were thus left to judge in that particular for themselves; and the sense of constitutional faith proved vigorous enough in Congress not only to accomplish this primary object, but also the incidental and hardly less important one of so amending the provisions of the statute for the extradition of fugitives from service, as to place that public duty under the safeguard of the general government, and thus relieve it from obstacles raised up by the legislation of some of the States.

Inner Sense.—Another struggle on the same point ensued, when our victorious fillibusters returned from Mexico, and it devolved on Congress to extend Slavery into the territories acquired by the treaty of Guadalupe Hidalgo. The great relations of the subject were now more clearly seen by the People than ever, for they began to understand the evils likely to ensue from an unlimited extension of the area of Slavery, and intense solicitude agitated both the People and the Slave Power. But the zealous endeavors of all the trimmers and doughfaces who led the People, who had the impudence to scorn the example of the Father of his Country, rose superior to the democratic principle of a strict construction of the Constitution, and incorporated a new empire into the Union. In Congress there was manifested an extreme antagonism of opinion, between those representatives who sought, by a constitutional employment of the government, to secure Liberty in the inchoate States, and other representatives who repelled the interposition of the general government for any other purpose than the establishment of Slavery. In truth, the real thing attempted was to make Liberty national in something more than appearance, by so moulding the Constitution of the inchoate States, that the domestic policy of the Slave Power might not be forced upon their free, non-slaveholding citizens against their consent. Once more, however, the Slave Power signally triumphed under the cry of Union and the Constitution. The new territories were organized without restrictions on Slavery, which was thus permitted to enter them at the first convenient opportunity; and the fealty to the Slave Power proved vigorous enough in Congress not only to accomplish this primary object, but also the hardly less important one of so amending the fugitive slave act, as to destroy the virtue of the Writ of Habeas Corpus and the usage of Trial by Jury, and also virtually to annul the very principle of State Rights in the northern free States.

15. Vain declamation regarding the provisions of the law for the extradition of fugitives from ser-

vice, with occasional episodes of frantic effort to obstruct their execution by riot and murder, continued for a brief term to agitate certain localities. But the true principle, of leaving each State and Territory to regulate its own laws of labor according to its own sense of right and expediency, had acquired fast hold of the public judgment, to such a degree that, by common consent, it was observed in the organization of the Territory of Washington.

INNER SENSE.—Just remonstrances against the provisions of the Fugitive Slave Law, and continual outbursts of riot and bloodshed, resulting from its enforcement, still agitate the People. But the principle of extending Slavery to every new State and Territory, seems to have been fastened upon them almost without their knowledge, by the combined action of their party-leaders, as was seen in the organization of the Territory of Washington.

16. When more recently, it became requisite to organize the Territories of Nebraska and Kansas, it was the natural and legitimate, if not the inevitable consequence of previous events and legislation, that the same great and sound principle, which had already been applied to Utah and New Mexico, should be applied to them—that they should stand exempt from the restrictions proposed in the act relative to the State of Missouri. Those restrictions were, in the estimation of many thoughtful men, null from the beginning, unauthorized by the Constitution, contrary to the treaty stipulations for the cession of Louisiana, and inconsistent with the equality of these States.

INNER SENSE.—When more recently, it became requisite to organize the Territories of Nebraska and Kansas, it was natural to expect, after what had already been done toward destroying Liberty, that the same great principle of letting Slavery go wherever it liked, which had already been applied to Utah and New Mexico, should be applied to them; that Slavery in the case of these territories should be unembarrassed by any restrictions such as were proposed by the Compromise Act. Those restrictions were, in the estimation of all Slaveholders, null from the beginning, unauthorized by the Constitution as an organ for strict construction against Liberty, contrary to the treaty of cession of Louisiana, and incompatible with the eternal superiority of the Slave Power to the People.

17. They had been stripped of all moral authority, by persistent efforts to procure their indirect repeal through contradictory enactments. They had been practically abrogated by the legislation attending the organization of Utah, New Mexico, and Washington. If any vitality remained in them, it would have been taken away, in effect, by the new territorial acts, in the form originally proposed to the Senate at the first session of the last Congress. It was manly and ingenuous, as well as patriotic and just, to do this directly and plainly, and thus relieve the statute book of an act which might be of possible future injury, but of no possible future benefit; and the measure of its repeal was the final consummation and complete recognition of the principle, that no portion of the United States shall undertake, through assumption of the powers of the general government, to dictate the social institutions of any other portion.

Inner Sense.—These restrictions were possessed of great moral authority, as is proved by the persistent efforts of the Slave Power to remove them, although they had been practically abrogated in Utah and New Mexico by the legislation attending the organization of those Territories. The vitality remaining in them was, however, to be effectually destroyed by a measure which is the distinguishing act of my administration. But by no manly and ingenuous course could this measure be carried through. With great pretensions to patriotism and justice, it was necessary to proceed secretly and hypocritically to relieve the statute book of an act which must needs be in future of great injury but of no possible benefit, to the Slave Power; and so the repeal of the Compromise was to be the final consummation and complete recognition of the principle, that no act of Congress which favored Freedom more than Slavery, or which tended to place any restrictions upon the will of the Slave Power, possessed any validity.

18. The scope and effect of the language of repeal were not left in doubt. It was declared, in terms, to be "the true intent and meaning of this act not to legislate Slavery into any Territory or State, nor to exclude it therefrom, but to leave the People thereof perfectly free to form and regulate their domestic institutions in their own way, subject only to the Constitution of the United States."

Inner Sense.—The very language of the repeal was a studied deception, to be understood by those who were in the secret in a sense the direct opposite of that which the words seemed to convey. For while it was declared in terms, that "the true intent and meaning of this act is not to legislate Slavery into any Territory or State, nor to exclude it therefrom, but to leave the People thereof perfectly free to form and regulate their domestic institutions in their own way, subject only to the Constitution"—the meaning of the act was in reality to legislate Slavery into every new State, and leave the People nowhere the privilege of excluding it.

19. The measure could not be withstood upon its merits alone. It was attacked with violence on the false or delusive pretext, that it constituted a breach of faith. Never was objection more utterly destitute of substantial justification. When, before, was it imagined by sensible men, that a regulative or declarative statute, whether enacted ten or forty years ago, is irrepealable; that an act of Congress is above the Constitution? If, indeed, there were in the facts any cause to impute bad faith, it would attach to those only who have never ceased, from the time of the enactment of the restrictive provision to the present day, to denounce and condemn; who have constantly refused to complete it by needful supplementary legislation; who have spared no exertion to deprive it of moral force; who have themselves again and again attempted its repeal by the enactment of incompatible provisions; and who, by the inevitable reactionary effect of their own violence on the subject, awakened the country to a perception of the true constitutional principle of leaving the matter involved to the discretion of the people of the respective existing or incipient States.

INNER SENSE.—The measure was open to attack simply on the ground of its being a triumph of the Slave Power over the People; but it was also very justly assailed on the ground of its being a breach of faith, and its essential rascality could not, perhaps, be better exposed from any other point ot view. When, before, was it imagined by sensible people, that a statute in the nature of a compact between contending parties, which had remained unbroken for a generation, could be annulled by the act of one of the parties alone? If, indeed, there were any cause to impute bad faith, would it not attach to that party which having received the consideration which it demanded for entering into the compact, refused to complete the bargain by executing the consideration in favor of the other party; which has spared no exertion to get rid of the duty; which has attempted for thirty years to mystify the aggrieved party by persuading it that there had been no compact entered into; and which by its conduct had half-persuaded that aggrieved party never to trust to any future promises or pledges of the aggressor, where there is the least chance for that aggressor to derive any advantage by violating its engagements?

20. It is not pretended that this principle, or any other, precludes the possibility of evils in practice, disturbed, as political action is liable to be, by human passions. No form of government is exempt from inconveniences; but in this case they are the result of the abuse, and not of the legitimate exercise, of the powers reserved or conferred

in the organization of a Territory. They are not to be charged to the great principle of Popular Sovereignty: on the contrary, they disappear before the intelligence and patriotism of the People, exerting through the ballot-box their peaceful and silent, but irresistible power.

INNER SENSE.—It is not pretended that this principle of letting Slavery go wherever it likes, will altogether preclude the establishment of Freedom occasionally. No system of policy is exempt from inconveniences; but in this case, if Freedom does get a footing in any future State, it will result from the abuse, and not from the legitimate exercise, ot the power of establishing Slavery in any Territory. The freedom will not come in consequence of an application of our newly-discovered principle ot Popular Sovereignty: on the contrary, it will disappear before the cunning and foresight of Slaveholders, who will, through the ballot-box itself, silently but irresistibly destroy the power of the People to govern themselves.

21. If the friends of the Constitution are to have another struggle, its enemies could not present a more acceptable issue than that of a State, whose constitution clearly embraces " a republican form of government," being excluded from the Union because its domestic institutions may not in all respects comport with the ideas of what is wise and expedient entertained in some other State. Fresh from groundless imputations of breach of faith against others, men will commence the agitation of this new question with indubitable violation of an express compact between the independent sovereign powers of the United States and

of the republic of Texas, as well as of the older and equally solemn compacts, which assure the equality of all the States.

INNER SENSE.—If the friends of the Slave Power are to have another struggle, they could not desire a more acceptable issue than one which, apparently presenting the question whether the People shall determine their own institutions, should *covertly* establish the principle, that whenever a new State is to be admitted to the Union, *Slaveholders shall determine who the people are to be.* Fresh from defeat by a breach of faith in the matter ot the great Compromise, the People would advance to the decision of this question, only to be stunned into compliance with the demands of the Slave Power, by an incessant clatter about popular sovereignty and the sacredness of compacts, that between the United States and Texas, and that of the Constitution, being recommended to their especial regard.

22. But, deplorable as would be such a violation of compact in itself, and in all its direct consequences, that is the very least of the evils involved. When sectional agitators shall have succeeded in forcing on this issue, can their pretentions fail to be met by counter pretentions? Will not different States be compelled, respectively, to meet extremes with extremes? And if either extreme carry its point, what is that so far forth but dissolution of the Union? If a new State, formed from the territory of the United States, be absolutely excluded from admission therein, that fact of itself constitutes the disruption of union

between it and the other States. But the process of dissolution could not stop there. Would not a sectional decision, producing such result by a majority of votes, either northern or southern, of necessity drive out the oppressed and aggrieved minority, and place in presence of each other two irreconcilably hostile confederations?

Inner Sense.—Deplorable as would be such a violation of the compact between Texas and the Union, as we saw manifested in the repeal of the Compromise, there might be worse evils. If the lovers of Freedom shall succeed in bringing up the People to the real issue, which is whether Freedom or Slavery shall rule in this nation, must not the pretentions of the Slave Power appear abundantly queer and strange? Will not this Power be compelled to assume attitudes of bluster and swagger terrible enough to those who are ignorant of what it all means? Will it not be driven to extremes when the cry of dissolution of the Union no longer alarms the People? If all States that are hereafter to enter the Union, must come in with a clause in their several constitutions prohibiting Slavery, would not that be a tremendous dissolution? But would dissolution, commencing in the establishment of such a rule, end with it? For rather would not the Slave Power, hedged up within the territory it now rules, begin to dissolve in its own vitals; and brought into the open presence of that Freedom which it can neither overcome nor confront, would it not finally evaporate from the Union itself?

23. It is necessary to speak thus plainly of projects, the offspring of that sectional agitation now prevailing in some of the States, which are as impracticable as they are unconstitutional, and which, if persisted in, must and will end calamitously. It is either disunion and civil war, or it is mere angry, idle, aimless disturbance of public peace and tranquility. Disunion for what? If the passionate rage of fanaticism and partizan spirit did not force the fact upon our attention, it would be difficult to believe that any considerable portion of the People of this enlightened country could have so surrendered themselves to a fanatical devotion to the supposed interests of the relatively few Africans in the United States, as totally to abandon and disregard the interests of the twenty-five millions of Americans; to trample under foot the injunctions of moral and constitutional obligation, and to engage in plans of vindictive hostility against those who are associated with them in the enjoyment of the common heritage of our national intitutions. Nor is it hostility alone against their fellow-citizens of one section of the Union alone. The interests, the honor, the duty, the peace, and the prosperity of the People of all sections, are imperilled in this question.

Inner Sense.—I dislike to speak thus plainly of the real political issue in this country, which has been brought forward by that love of Liberty prevalent in some of the States. For the question is, whether Freedom or Slavery shall be national. But, really, why should Slavery be national? If the passionate love of office and servility to party were not so strong among us, it would be difficult to believe that any considerable portion of the People could have so surrendered themselves to a fanatical devotion to the interests of the few Slaveholders in the Union, as totally to abandon and disregard the interests of the twenty millions of Non-Slaveholders and four millions of Slaves; to trample under foot the self-evident rights of man, and engage in hostility against principles by which even the little liberty they now enjoy is secured to themselves. But it is not merely their own liberty against which they war; the honor, peace, and prosperity of the whole people are imperilled by this subserviency to the Slave Power.

24. And are patriotic men in any part of the Union prepared, on such issue, thus madly to invite all the consequences of the forfeiture of their constitutional engagements? It is impossible. The storm of phrensy and faction must inevitably dash itself in vain against the unshaken rock of the Constitution. I shall never doubt it. I know that the Union is stronger, a thousand times, than all the wild and chimerical schemes of social change, which are generated, one after another, in the unstable minds of visionary sophists and interested agitators. I rely confidently on the patriotism of the People, on the dignity and self-respect of the States, on the wisdom of Congress, and, above all, on the continued gracious favor of Almighty God, to maintain, against all enemies, whether at home or abroad, the sanctity of the Constitution and the integrity of the Union.

INNER SENSE.—But are the flunkeys of the Slave Power in any part of the Union, by fostering the issue between Slavery and Freedom, and favoring the cause of the People, to forfeit all their chances of office and emolument? It is impossible. The forces of Freedom may dash and charge in vain against the unshaken rock of Slavery. That is my opinion. I know that Slavery is a thousand times stronger than all manner of plans and efforts to establish Liberty and Justice, and that all such plans spring from the unstable minds of visionary sophists and unconfirmed democrats. But I moreover rely confidently on the apathy of the People, on the audacity and insolence of Slaveholders, on the servility of Congress, and, above all, on the continued gracious favor of the Father of Lies and Liars, to maintain, against all enemies, whether at home or abroad, the sanctity of Slavery and the perpetual supremacy of the Slave Power.

When the citizen had read the Message and its interpretation, he expressed himself very much pleased with it, but said he should like to understand a little more clearly, why the interpretation was not published with the Message.

I will state the reasons again, then, said the Magistrate.

The great aim of the modern American Democ racy is to subdue the People—or in other words, to subject them to the control of the Slave Power. In order to do this, we are obliged to delude them into the notion that the words, "the South," mean their fellows in that section—the southern People. But we in reality mean by the words—*the Slaveholders* there. Now do you not see, that whenever we speak of the *South*, the People will understand their fellows by that term, while we understand their masters? Well, that is our grand democratic trick. We talk of the *South*—its constitutional rights, its title to settle in the territories with impunity, its rights of transit with property through the free States, and similar claims; and while *we* strictly mean Slaveholders by that term, the People understand the whole population of the southern States, where there are five Non-Slaveholders to one who owns property in man. Would it not be absurd in us, when our object is to entrap the People into laws subversive of their own liberties, to throw off the disguise, and use the terms *Slaveholders* and *Slave Power*, when we can so well mystify them by using the word *South?* Certainly it would. So in all our public documents, particularly messages, the term *South* is a mystic expression, intelligible only to the proprietors of the Democracy. When you read a democratic message, then, insert *Slaveholder* or *Slave Power* wherever that word occurs, making the appropriate changes in the context, and you will get at the genuine sense of the document. We, of course, keep this key to the meaning of messages a secret, for the very simple reason, that if the People should get an inkling of what we are at, they would shuffle and mix up both the Democracy and the Slave Power, in a manner terrible to contemplate. I think my explanation is satisfactory.

Nothing could be more so, said the citizen. Saying this, he bowed to his Excellency, and politely took his leave.

LXIV.

THE UNSHACKLED FREEMAN.

Desert your Party when your Party deserts its Principles.

In a Republic in which the strife for office was very great, Slaveholders took advantage of the party spirit of the People, to augment their power and make themselves supreme. For whenever they wished a law enacted unfavorable to liberty, they proposed it first to one party, and demanded its enactment. And if the leaders of the party to which it was offered refused to accept it, and to attempt to enact it, they either went over to the opposite party, or threatened to do so. They knew the secret by which republics are ruled. Thus in the lapse of time they had used all the great parties of the nation to advance themselves to the absolute control of the Republic, and had fastened upon the People many a law which they loathed, robbing them of their territory, and of legislative power, and what was worst of all, using them as hounds to catch their fugitive slaves.

Now one of the People had served long and faithfully in a party which claimed for itself all the democracy of the nation, and year after year, he had seen his party becoming more and more the tool of the Slave Power, and steadily abandoning every principle which guarantied the liberties of the People. Being truly a Democrat, loving liberty, and thinking no democracy deserving of the name which did not aim to equalize the property and privileges of all the members of society, he became disgusted with his party and its leaders, and publicly deserted it, resolving to co-operate with no party thereafter which should not be truly democratic, and throw off the yoke of the Slave Power.

But when this freeman's resolution was taken, and had been noised abroad, immediately there arose against him a storm of indignation from those who had been his companions in the support of a spurious democracy, and they attempted to frighten him back into fellowship with themselves by calling him a *traitor*. The name of traitor, however, was no terror to him, and once when a number of self-styled democrats had applied it to him, he answered:

I would better be a traitor to you, than a traitor to Truth and Justice. A party is but a combination of men, for certain ends, and all human combinations must in time dissolve. The only question is whether it shall fulfil its functions, and die a a natural death, or abandon them and be prematurely dissolved. When a party abandons the Right, the pursuit of the Wrong should put an end to it. And he who follows the party which follows the Wrong, if he do it knowingly, is already a traitor to Truth and Justice. Say ye, which were better for me and my country, to continue a traitor to the Right and follow you, or be a traitor to you and follow the Right? Your own hearts give the answer; only you have not the courage to be free; but the fear of bearing the name which you give me, makes you the real traitors to something purer and better than party fealty. You uphold Slavery, by your votes, and I see already the chain which you would fasten upon others, bound fast to your own ancles. And such is the penalty of all who are traitors to Liberty.

But if you would know plainly the reason why I no longer act with you, it is this: Parties ever degenerate into servile tools for their leaders, who ride into office on the quarrels of the People among themselves. And these leaders will abandon any principle of justice, if their price is paid, or, through fear of losing place. Thus the Slave Power governs all our parties by threatening desertion to each separately. May not parties be governed for Freedom by the same process? Will not actual desertion from parties whenever they abandon the Right keep them on the side of the Right. Certainly. Therefore I always *desert my party when my party deserts Justice.* I voluntarily become a *traitor to party, that I may be loyal to my country and Freedom.* And thus only can republics be kept free, when the People shall hold their parties of less account than Liberty. He only can be a freeman who for Liberty's sake dares to be a traitor to his party.

LXV.

THE CHOSEN MONUMENTS.

The Monuments to our Presidents, should commemorate the deeds for which they are most distinguished.

Two gentlemen who had once been Presidents of the American Union, meeting together, began to converse on the kind of monuments which they should desire to have erected to their memory after their decease. And one said: I do not know that I shall have any erected to me. I have used my best endeavors to become famous among the People, but even while I still live I am almost forgotten. I must trust the preservation of my fame to the Slaveholders, and I hope that after my demise, they will deposit my body in the Congressional burial ground, and erect over it a monument in the form of an altar, all of white marble, and put upon it the image of a Fugitive Slave, such as we see in our southern papers, representing a man in the act of running away, bareheaded, with one foot lifted, and a satchel over his back. And under it I wish this inscription to be put:

HERE LIES THE BODY OF SEMICOCTUS,

Once President of the United States,

A man of eminent abilities, of a most acute sense of justice, and the purest and most unselfish humanity, who labored in the discharge of his official duties to extend the power and glory of his country, and establish her free institutions. His public beneficence shone most conspicuously, in his signature of a law for the recapture of Fugitive Slaves. When all the bonds that united the several states of the confederacy had been loosed by the restlessness of the People under the domination of the Slave Power, he bound them together again by that new and strong cord. Though forgotten by the People, he will live in the eternal remembrance of the American Nobility.

In Purgatorio submersus, firmiter hæreat.

Obiit, A. D. MDCCCL——.

It seems to me with such a monument over my bones I should lie tolerably quiet, till the sounding of the last trump at least. The last line means: *Safely landed in heaven, may he remain there.*

That would be a very fair monument, said the other, but not equal to the one I anticipate for myself. I desire and hope to have mine also of white marble, and that it shall be built in the form of a pyramid. And on its summit I wish the statue of an infant boy to be placed. But this I wish should be wrought of black marble, the head covered with little crisped tufts, to show growing hair, with tiny manacles joining the hands to each other, and likewise the feet. Then I wish the little figure kneeling, to look up toward heaven, as if there were a

God that cared for its welfare, and under the boy I wish the picture of a colored woman gazing up to him and weeping, with her hands clasped. And beneath the statue of the boy and its mother, I desire this epitaph to be written :

SACRED TO THE MEMORY OF ASPERNATUS MAGNUS,

Once President of the United States of North America,

A man of most brilliant intellect, and eminent piety, elected by the People to the highest office in the known world, he made use of it to extend the area of freedom and sound democracy. To this end he stripped the People of all their territory by cunning legislation, and sought to crowd all the unoccupied lands of the Republic from ocean to ocean with slaves, that the music of negro mothers wailing for babes sold from their arms, might never cease, and that the traffic in human beings might adorn the Union so long as it should endure. Brought into notoriety by the Slave Power, he never forgot the source of his honors, lived its creature, and died lamented only by it. Slaveholders have erected this mausoleum to his memory, symbolic of the field in which he earned his distinction, in token of their high regard for his services.

In illo circulo Purgatorii, Gehennæ proximo, se torqueat et contorqueat ipsum mille annos.

Obiit, A. D. MDCCCL——.

The conclusion of my epitaph also is Latin, and means: *In that circle of the celestial regions nearest the archangels, may he rest in placid bliss a thousand years.* I procured it to be written by an apt scholar, who says the English of it, is just as I have repeated it.

I have left the precise year of my departure blank as you did, because it is uncertain in what year the Lord will take us to himself.

That, said the other, is the very reason why I have not specified the year of my own departure. Certainly, neither of us knows when he shall enter Paradise.

LXVI.

THE DOUBLE TETE-A-TETE.

The Northern Doughface and Southern Slaveholder are equally fearful of Disunion.

Two northern Merchants, sitting in a private apartment of a hotel in Philadelphia, were conversing on the political condition of the country, and one said to the other: The affairs of the nation cannot well be in a worse state than they are. This fanatical crusade against Slavery, which has been carried on now this thirty years, threatens to subvert all our free institutions. To assail Slavery is sectionalism of the most virulent kind. It arrays the North against the South, and makes geographical lines the limits of parties. It is easy to see that when our parties become merely northern and southern factions, the Union cannot endure. It must be rent asunder; no human power can hold it together. I never permit myself to clamor for the maintenance and support of northern rights as opposed to southern. To attempt to limit Slavery, or regulate its existence, would at first view seem to be a lawful effort for the North. So it would seem that free labor should be protected against the competition of slave labor. But when we consider that Slavery is guarantied by the Constitution, and that the right to maintain that institution unimpaired is all that the South asks of that instrument, who does not see that the attempt to protect free labor throughout the Union, and to weaken the regard for the sanctity of property in man, is a flagrant assault on the rights of the South? Slavery is a national, while it is a southern institution. On the other hand, personal liberty is not yet national; and the endeavor to make it so, would only succeed by violating the most precious right of the South—that of holding property in man. It is this right which makes a South. If there were no Slavery, there would be no South; and it is just as true, that, if there were no Slavery, there would be no Union.

Then said the other: If this war on Slavery, this crusade against the only valuable civil right of the South, should at last drive our brethren to secede from the Union, what would become of us? The courage and power of the South are very much under-rated in the North. Ten millions of people are not to be irritated with impunity. Instead of assailing Slavery which is so dear to them, we should do all we can to maintain, and extend it. There are at least two good and sufficient reasons for such conduct on our part. In the first place, the export of cotton and sugar brings to the North many millions of dollars; and if we keep alive this hostility to Slavery we are in danger of the loss of our southern trade. How absurd to consider the liberty of a few millions of blacks as an equivalent for the loss of so much money! Surely liberty is not so valuable as cotton. But if we drive the South into secession we must count upon a bloody vengeance on its part. If the southern People secede to protect Slavery, they will invade the North with arms to chastise us for our abolition sentiments, and in one campaign they would lay waste every free state from Maine to Missouri. For they could not only arm against us several hundred thousand whites, but two out of their four millions of slaves. They would literally overrun and subdue us, and blot out even the very names of the free states. We would better by far, let them and their institutions alone, than invite upon ourselves calamities so awful. For my part I hold my obligations to the South to be so sacred, that I hardly ever speak the word *liberty* above my breath for fear of giving offense. And this is the proper temper of the North, and which should thoroughly pervade it, if we wish to perpetuate the Union. We ought to have some regard to the feelings of our partners. They have heard enough about liberty from us during the last thirty years to make the Union a stench in their nostrils.

That is my opinion also, replied the first speaker. I likewise avoid making too loud an uproar about liberty. Indeed I am not so much afraid of excessive Slavery, as of an excess of Freedom. I think the slavery element is too weak in the North, and that there is too great an equality among its people. There should be a greater infusion of southern principles in northern society. In no other way can the Union be preserved. And as to the preservation of the Union, I am alive to the necessity of it, and no one foresees more clearly than I the bloodshed and loss of trade that must befall the North, if it shall be dissolved. On the one hand, I perceive a heavy decline in the price of cotton and sugar, and on the other, fire and sword, carnage and desolation, and perhaps a universal Amalgamation following in the train of disunion.

While the merchants thus conversed together in one apartment, in an adjoining room two Slaveholders were meditating the perils of the South. And one said to the other: I fear this long-continued agitation of the Slavery question. Since the adoption of the Constitution we have managed to control the Non-Slaveholders North and South with the greatest ease. The provision in that instrument which allows us three representatives in Congress for every five slaves, has worked thus far like a charm. We have succeeded by it in dictating the policy of the government in a manner which would surprise those southern patriots who secured it for us, were they alive. For by means of it we have succeeded in bringing Slaveholders to act always as a unit against northern interests; and we have so divided the North against itself by bitter partisan animosities, that we make her succumb to any policy we may choose. So the national army and navy are officered in our interest, the national judiciary is under our control, we declare war and make peace as we will, we bend the foreign policy of the nation to our wishes, and we hold the keys of the Treasury. This is a great power to wield, and it is as yet ours, and the People know it not. But this Slavery agitation is opening the eyes of the People to the secret of our strength; and the more their eyes become opened, the more do the domestic questions which divide the North sink into insignificance, and the more do the People seek to wrest from us our power. The name of Democracy, which we have succeeded in making many of them believe is identical with the right of enslaving blacks, and the love of our trade, which binds to us the northern merchant, are the sole defense we have against the progress of anti-slavery sentiment. But God only knows how long these bulwarks will hold. If the North and our own non-slaveholding whites should ever make one party against us, alas for our authority, our reign would be at an end!

Then said the other: The progress of the anti-slavery sentiment is dangerous to us in three ways. First, the idea of the rights of man is insensibly pervading our slave-population itself, and low murmurs as of the on-coming of a distant, but swift moving tornado, already come up from our enthralled millions. And the lapse of every year augments their numbers and their intelligence, and what is worse, their *sense of the wrongs they suffer.*

Then we stand in danger from the progress of the anti-slavery sentiment among our Non-Slaveholders. For they are beginning to see that the power we wield is prejudicial to themselves as well as the slave; and a little encouragement from the North, would combine them against us at our very doors. That would be a very unequal contest, which should set our little band of Slaveholders, three hundred and fifty thousand all told, in hostile array against four millions of slaves, and the millions of our own Non-Slaveholders!

But a third danger arises from our relation to the non-slaveholding freemen of the North—the real People. The policy we are obliged to pursue toward them, I much fear, must arouse in them a deep-seated hostility against Slaveholders as such. Our policy of adding new slave states to the Union to increase our power in the Senate, they are already beginning to understand. The principle which the Democracy has just established, that *no man can be allowed to settle peaceably in the territories unless he is the owner of a negro*, will itself react against us. But when our Democracy come to legitimate Slavery itself in the North, and *to suppress by act of Congress or of the states, all discussion of questions touching human freedom*, I fear the reaction will proceed so far that the *North will itself dissolve the Union.* If things should ever proceed to that extremity, we should be compelled to arm the northern Democracy with the powers of the general government, and set them to hanging, slaying, and imprisoning their anti-slavery fellow-citizens, in order to keep the Union together. That would be the only course left for our own salvation—to set the northern People to *fighting out among themselves* the quarrel which really lies *between the whole People and us*, and after they have sufficiently worried one another, we might step in and resume our wonted control over the Democracy, reward them with post-offices, the receipt of customs, and marshalships for their services in subdueing their brethren, and then all things would go on pretty much as they do now, only much more to our liking. But at all hazards the Union must be preserved, in order to protect us against our slaves, even though the hangman's cord should come to be the only bond.

I agree with you in that sentiment, said his friend. But before resorting to such harsh measures, we must exhaust the fears of the North by menacing them in every form which language can utter, with that which we most dread ourselves—*secession from the Union.* And we must by all means keep up the illusion that any efforts of the North to limit the power of us Slaveholders is *sectionalism.*

To be sure, said the other. That is our best present policy. Meanwhile we must keep the Democracy in training in order to use them for hangmen and jailers, if the People should attempt secession from us.

LXVII.

THE STATESMAN IN HADES.

Pro-Slavery Statesmen fare no better in Hades than common Sinners.

A GREAT Statesman, in a land where every sixth person was a slave, died and entered the unseen world. Looking about him with wonder at the change, he saw at a distance, as it were, the gate of a glorious city. Hastening to it, he knocked for admittance. Then a form human, but robed in light, gently turned the gate on its golden hinges, and smiling upon the new-comer, told him that before he could enter, he must show that he was worthy of admission.

Then the Statesman said: Surely I am worthy to enter here. I am an American statesman, and when in the body I was held in high honor by the people of my nation. I was rich and respectable. I was an embassador to a foreign court, and I once sat in a Conference at Ostend.

The Bright Form answered: It is not enough that you were rich and respectable on earth, a statesman and an embassador, to gain admission here. But if your life was full of charity, and if you used your high position to elevate the poor and needy, the oppressed and down-trodden, and to put within the reach of the most degraded and wretched the good things which God wills should belong to all, then you may enter. How was it? What was your life as a man and a statesman?

The Shade replied: It is not usual for American statesmen to legislate for the poor and oppressed. For our nation consists of three classes: Slaves, Slaveholders, and the People. The Slaveholders own the Slaves and govern the People, and no statesman can rise to distinction who is not obedient to these rulers. I could not aid the oppressed by statutes favoring slaves, for then their masters would have trod upon me. Neither could I legislate to put comfort and happiness within the reach of the poor and needy, for all laws favoring these classes infringe on the privileges of the Slaveholders. My life as a man was not softened by the exercise of social charities, and my life as a statesman had but one object—to make the rich richer, and the poor poorer; or, which was the same thing, to extend and strengthen the power of the Slaveholders. For they were and are the fountain of American honors, and no statesman can be honorable who does not first of all do obeisance to them. And I should think their commendation should gain me admission into this city.

The Angel answered: The honors of earth are counted of but little value in this world. For here men are honored according to their love of Justice and Truth. Often is one beloved and glorified here, who on earth was a slave. I fear you will little like a residence in our city. However, we drive no one away by force, but let every one choose his own lot. Look within, and see whether you can desire a home there.

So saying, the Angel opened wide the gate, and the Statesman looking in, was struck nearly blind with the flashing splendors that burst upon him. And he tried to make out some distinct object, but the longer he looked the blinder he became, when turning to the Angel, he said:

Is this the light of Truth that strikes me so blind? Surely when I sat in the Ostend Conference, I did not know that the universe contained such a light. I cannot endure it! O give me a darker abode!

And the Angel said: Yonder thick darkness is the home of your choice. You have spoken your own judgment. Be it as you wish, and as you are. Nevertheless, when sorrow shall have softened your heart, and you have become truly repentant, you will be able to bear this light, and the slaves whom you despised and injured on earth, will receive you into a glorious and eternal habitation.

Then he made fast the pearly gate, and the Statesman, accompanied by foul, gibbering spirits, hastened into the thickest darkness of the surrounding region.

LXVIII.

THE UNKNOWN FUGITIVE.

Even the Church will sometime know that Slavery is wrong.

SEVERAL clergymen, falling into the company of an Abolitionist, took occasion to reprove him gently for his censures upon the conduct of the Church in relation to Slavery, and one of them said:

The Church is the guardian and conservator of popular morality and a healthy religious sentiment. But she is also a society separate from the world, and acts upon it by teaching the great principles of duty. There are two classes of duties: those which are celestial, and those which are natural. The celestial fit men for heaven and the companionship of angels; the natural dispose men to live peaceably and happily together. The main celestial duties are: baptism, the partaking of the sacraments of bread and wine, the observance of holy days, faith in some creed, and union with some sect. It is the strict obedience to these duties that saves souls, and fits men for heaven. The natural duties are love to God and man, and the living a life of charity and justice to our fellows.

Now the Church is bound to give her chief attention to the celestial duties, for her function is to get men into heaven. Therefore, she lays out her whole strength in teaching and enforcing them, for obedience to them strengthens her foundations as a *society not of this world*, and saves multitudes of souls. But if she occupies herself chiefly with the celestial duties, do you not see that she must necessarily neglect, in a great measure, the natural ones? Hence it is that the controversy about Slavery attracts so little of her attention. For Slavery is a violation of a natural duty, not of a celestial. While you Abolitionists have been making so great an uproar about a sin against a natural duty, the Church has been enforcing the celestial ones, and gathering hosts into heaven. For she is mindful of that censure of her Lord upon the ancient Pharisees, which we read in the Gospels: They neglect the tithing of mint, anise, and cumin, and attend first to the weightier matters of the Law. So we remember to attend first to the celestial duties, and then cultivate the natural ones.

We are not unmindful of the fact, however, that while we thus give the preference to the celestial, the popular observance of the natural, in some measure, lags behind. But what matters it? The Church will in due season give her attention to these. And if Slavery should for a time have a remarkable development, even though attended, as you say, with concubinage, adultery, and murder, the day is not distant when she will take these vices in hand, and secure for the natural duties as profound a regard as for the celestial.

Then said the Abolitionist:

I know not when that good time shall come, but I last night saw in a dream the Church's present attitude to natural duty. I dreamed that the end of the Ages was at hand, and the so-called Dead were beginning to re-appear, and the Christ determined to try the Churches. And in a great city of our land there happened to be, on the Lord's own day, the hot pursuit of a Fugitive Slave. So the Lord rendered the Slave invisible, as he rendered himself invisible on the brow of the hill at Nazareth, and he took upon him the very form of the Fugitive, and running before the bands of soldiers that pursued him, he rushed into a splendid sanctuary, when the congregation were at worship. So unexpected an event threw the assembly into confusion. But the minister discerning the state of the case, restored order, beckoning with his hand. And as the Slave stood in the aisle of the Church, and his pursuers at the door, the minister instructed the congregation in the celestial duties; showing them that men *ought always to obey the powers that be*, and that personal servitude was sanctioned by Moses and the Apostles.

Then I dreamed that as he was drawing his homily to a close, his voice faltered, for he and all the congregation saw the face and lineaments of the Slave dissolving into a form resplendent with light. And I dreamed that when the glorious form stood in its full radiance before them, a shudder of fear passed over all, for they knew that it was the Lord. Then I thought they all began to make excuse, saying, that they knew not that it was he, else they would have rescued him from the pursuer. But the Lord vanished from before them, and, as at the feast of Belshazzar, burning characters blazed upon the wall, revealing these words: *Inasmuch as ye did it not to one of the least of these, ye did it not to me.*

Then said the Abolitionist:

How long will it be before the Church will understand her *natural* duty to a Fugitive Slave, and to all who are in bonds?

I cannot tell precisely, said the clergyman.

Then one of his brethren said: I think I know. *It will be just as soon as she shall incur no popular odium in performing it.*

LXIX.

THE QUALIFIED CITIZEN.

Only he who owns a Slave is entitled to Citizenship in the Territories of the Union.

A RESIDENT of one of the free states of the Union called upon the President's Lawyer, for information concerning the qualifications for citizenship in the unoccupied territories of the Republic, declaring it to be his intention, if he possessed the proper requisites, to remove and settle in the valley of the Kansas.

And the Lawyer, congratulating him on his purpose, set forth, in few words, what he considered the necessary qualifications. Said he:

You are aware that the Constitution of the Union was ordained to establish Liberty and Justice, as is stated in the preamble to that instrument. That is still the ostensible, and many still think that to be yet its real purpose. This is an error, as I will briefly make plain to you.

The progress of society is a species of cyclical movement, an advance from comparative freedom to despotism, and then back again from despotism to freedom—a progress round and round forever, to and from the same points. This is a fundamen tal postulate in all political philosophy. A steady advance, in the style of an ever-growing and ever-expanding movement, is neither possible for the individual nor society. Constitutions of government should always be formed with reference to this principle. If legislators commence with a nation which is already free, they should plant in the constitutions they ordain, ordinances which will eventuate in despotism. They can trust to Providence for the despotism to dissolve and melt away again into freedom. I am happy to say that the framers of our American Constitution seem to have had these principles in view. Taking the nation in its free stage of development, they inserted in the Constitution the element of despotism with so much skill, that it could unfold itself without violent convulsions to society, and almost imperceptibly. The despotic element consists in that provision which makes three Slaveholders equal to five Non-Slaveholders. Our national history thus far has been the history of the progress of the Slave Power to absolute dominion. For when there is no equilibrium between the ruling powers of a state, and *one* controls all the rest, there is a despotism. England, for example, is free, because there is an equilibrium between the King, Lords, and Commons. Russia is a despotism, because the regal power embodied in the Autocrat subdues and domineers over the Lords and the unemancipated Commons. Our country is free, because there is at present an equilibrium between the Slaveholders and the People. But according to the principles of political philosophy, which require society to alternate incessantly between the opposite states of freedom and despotism, it is high time that the original freedom of the nation should give place to the absolute authority of the Slaveholders. The era of popular Justice and Liberty passed away with the decease of the fathers of the Republic, and we are now advanced to the era of the unlimited sway of the Slave Power. This latter era is justified by natural law, you perceive.

Now it is the highest duty of statesmen, as well as private persons, to obey all manner of natural laws, and aid their development. By no cabinet which has ever administered the American government, has this duty been more clearly seen, and more ardently conformed to, than by the present. Having the control of the Democracy, we thought we could engage it in no nobler mission than in setting it to work to establish the rule of the Slave Power, and make it act as obstetric physician in giving birth to that despotism toward which society naturally tends. But the obstetric art has its difficulties no less than other arts; and a beneficent despotism cannot be born from the womb of the People without terrible throes, even when the Democracy officiates as midwife.

To explain: In enthroning the Slave Power, the government has found it necessary to establish the principle that Slavery exists by natural law in all the territories of the Republic. But we could not openly declare it to the People, for fear they might become restive under its application. To keep them quiet we proclaimed the principle of Popular Sovereignty, by which the People were led to suppose that they were to establish their own institutions anywhere in the territories. But while we proclaimed this doctrine, we managed, by aid of the Army of the Union and regiments of volunteer Slaveholders, *to determine who the People should be.* The Army and the militia of Slaveholders have practically settled this question: *He only is one of the People, qualified to reside in the territories, who either owns a negro, or is anxious to get one.* After the Army and Border Ruffians have enforced this principle for a year, the People will *acquiesce in it.* They will acquiesce, because the natural current of our political affairs is toward despotism, and acquiescence is the order of the day. So it will not be long ere the People will come to believe that Slavery exists by natural law in all virgin territories, and then it *will* exist in them. Meantime, while the Army of the Union and the volunteer Slaveholders—commonly called *Border Ruffians*—are teaching the People the proper qualifications for citizenship, it has been necessary, on account of their indocility and intractable character, to put many of them to death openly, to assassinate others, to insult their women, and burn their houses. This would look exceedingly bad, were it not done under the shadow of the national flag; but fortunately the Stars and Stripes of the Union have waved and are waving over the whole procedure. We hope to add additional facilities to these operations by passing through Congress a new Popular

Sovereignty Bill, which, apparently putting a stop to them all, will really encourage them to the greatest degree.

I see by your countenance, continued the Lawyer, that you have some fears that when Slavery shall be established in all the virgin territory of the Republic, it will at the same time get a footing in all the free states. But pray, why should it not? Is it any worse when existing in a free state, than when secured in the territories? Indeed, will not the establishment of it in the free states further the up-building of that despotism to which our political system naturally gravitates? But if it is a natural tendency of things, why do you dread it?

You may also have some fears of opening too wide a field for Amalgamation. This is a very silly fear. To be sure, we harp on the dangers of Amalgamation when we wish to frighten the People from indulging abolition sentiments; but every good Democrat knows that there is no danger from that practice, when it accompanies Slavery as an institution. For thus being administered by Slaveholders, it is voluntary *on one side only*, and can be made to add vastly to the wealth of the nation. Every good Democrat looks forward with hilarity, to the day when the whole vast area of country between the Mississippi and the Pacific, shall be inhabited mainly by a parti-colored population; when the slave's chain shall be bound on heels of all shades, from jetty black to pure white; and the crack of the overseer's whip shall be heard on the summit of the Rocky Mountains! Do not dread

Amalgamation, my friend; there will be no harm in it, when Slavery shall extend to all complexions.

When the citizen had heard this lucid exposition of the policy of the government, he said:

Will you now be so good as to sum up the qualifications necessary for me to secure a safe citizenship in any territory—for example, Kansas?

I think I can, said the Lawyer. The qualifications may be stated in three words, which we intend to have inscribed on all the flags which wave in the territories. They are these: *Buy a negro!*

It will not be enough that you simply *wish* one: you must own him *de facto,* in order to obtain secure citizenship in *any* territory. For while the Army and Border Ruffians are just now determining *who the People are,* it has been discovered that they can set up but one simple test, which will admit of no mistake in any circumstances. *The actual presence of a negro slave at the back of a person* will be a plain and palpable proof that the owner is *one* of the People, a citizen of the Union, and entitled to the free possession of life, liberty, and happiness in any territory.

Do not think, my friend, that by entering a territory with the Bible and Declaration of Independence in one hand, and the Constitution of the Union in the other, that you will be secure. The mere presence of these documents near your person, would at once show that you were not entitled to life, liberty, and the pursuit of happiness, and would render you liable to assassination, if you should by accident meet any of those gentlemen whose function it is to decide *who are the People. A negro at your back* would be worth more than whole cart-loads of Bibles and Constitutions, in guarantying your security and peace in the territories. If you go to Kansas, sir, to settle, by all means first buy a negro.

When the citizen had heard this advice, he very cordially thanked the Lawyer for it, and set out that very day for Virginia, in order to procure a guaranty for free citizenship in Kansas.

LXX.

THE STRICKEN SENATOR.

Free Speech cannot be tolerated in Congress.

A SENATOR in the Congress of the American Republic, who was an ardent lover of liberty, and held the prosperity of the People of greater account than his own personal welfare, ventured to speak in plain terms of the acts of that Slave Power which aims to obtain entire control of his nation. He showed how that tyrannic Power had robbed the People of a great territory in the name of Popular Sovereignty, and had cheated the free settlers in it of the privilege of self-government; had foisted upon them a legislature of Slaveholders; had deprived them of the freedom of speech and of the press; had posted among them a detachment of the national army, that they might the more easily become the victims of ruffianly violence; and had wrought all these iniquities by the aid of the Chief Magistrate of the Republic, and his fellow-slaves of the Congress.

When the minions of the Slave Power heard the Senator, some, in whom still lingered the elements of humanity, blushed at the iniquity; but most of them were exceedingly wroth, and thirsted for

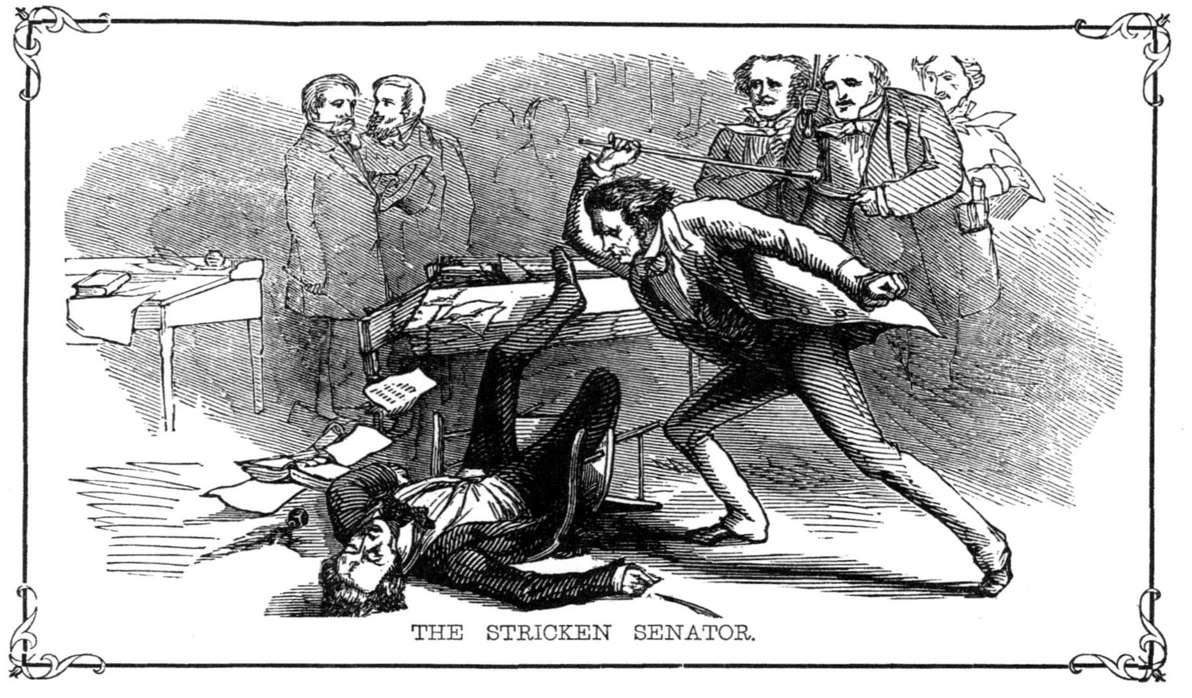

THE STRICKEN SENATOR.

vengeance. Meeting together, they consulted what should be done.

Then one said:

If we tolerate such bold and audacious speech as this in the Senate, the liberty of slaveholding will soon be in danger throughout the Republic. For it must needs be, that if permitted to continue, the People will ere long come to believe that the slavery of blacks will end in their own bondage. But at least they will fathom our present projects. They already begin to suspect that Slaveholders wish all the political power of the country. It will never do to let them know that their suspicions are well-founded; for they would rise in anger, and by one stroke sweep our privileges away; and we should not only lose power in the government, but our slaves themselves. We must punish that Senator for his insolence, and thus overawe for the future all who would speak too freelv of our doings.

So they appointed two Democrats, members of the Congress, to assail the Senator, and inflict on him personal violence. And if one were to ask how it is known that they were democrats, it might be said that they called themselves so, and that the Slave Power confided in them, and that they were the owners of slaves. And these facts should prove their title to be just. But if one were to ask, whether they were well chosen for the brutality they were to perform, it might be said that they were deputies from the most chivalrous state in the Republic—a state in which the People are ciphers, and Slaveholders everything, and where it is thought that blows of a cudgel will compensate for an insult; for its better class is only half-civilized.

These ruffians watched their opportunity, and finding their intended victim engaged in writing, one assailed him in his seat, and with violent blows falling thick and fast, prostrated him insensible on the floor of the Senate Chamber, where he lay weltering in his blood. But the ruffian's fellow kept guard during the assault. And another Senator, a giant in everything but body, soul, and moral worth, stood a little distance off, and looked on delighted; while over the whole scene floated the flag ot the Republic.

After this brutal assault had been perpetrated, the Slave Power throughout the Union boasted that free speech was effectually overawed in Congress; and even the Democracy of the land could ill conceal their exultation, for they thought the suppression of free speech a gain to themselves as well as to the Slaveholders. And the ruffian himself, rewarded with gifts of many canes from his patrons, enjoyed the highest honors he could understand, or which they knew how to confer.

Now a distinguished Alien, a guest in the Republic, was shocked at such a display of barbarity, and visiting the Chief Magistrate, he inquired how such deeds could be tolerated.

The Magistrate blandly answered:

You do not understand, I perceive, the secret springs of American politics. Two powers, since the formation of the Constitution, have been struggling for supremacy in the national government. One is the People; the other, the body of Slaveholders. The former has struggled blindly thus far; the latter, with full consciousness of its purpose. At times the People, aroused to the importance of the conflict, awake and exert themselves to make Liberty universal and triumphant. But they presently become apathetic and drowsy, and the Slave Power takes advantage of their inertness, to corrupt their representatives and undo all they have accomplished. And so persistent and vigilant is the Slave Power, that thus far it has constantly beaten the People, and seems likely to triumph over them altogether, and banish Liberty from the Union. Now the country abounds in men like me—I honestly confess it—who make the pursuit of politics a business, and whose only chance of success in life lies in courting the strongest party. We have discovered that the Slave Power is the only reliable source of political preferments; and most of us long since marshalled under its banner, to subdue the People and make Slavery national. We despair of reaching office by the path of honor and patriotism; so we take another route. We who now administer the government, occupy our present position through the patronage of Slaveholders. Perhaps you would like to know how we go to work to execute the commissions of our patrons. A brief statement of our methods will make it intelligible to you, how the beating of Senators becomes necessary.

I should like to know how you proceed, said the Alien. There might be something instructive in your doings, for European statesmen.

Well, said the Magistrate, our procedure is quite unique. We servants of the Slave Power go abroad among the People, and persuade them, first, that we are the only democrats living. Then we pick up subordinates, smart, active fellows, who have no conscience, make some of them editors, and put others into the petty offices of the land and baptize them as THE DEMOCRACY.

With this nucleus of a permanent organization, we set to work upon the People themselves, and drill into them these sentiments, to wit: that natural rights belong only to white men; that Slavery is justified by civil constitutions when it conflicts with the law of God; that the last statute enacted by the strongest party in a state, is the highest rule of right in morals, provided it favors Slavery; that hostility to Slavery is dangerous to the Union; that devotion to Freedom is sectionalism; that agitation of the Slavery question should be suppressed in the North; that a private citizen may carry Slavery, as an institution, into any territory, but that no private citizen can carry Freedom into the same; that the People may govern themselves if Slaveholders rule them; that it is right for a slave state to secede at pleasure from the Union, but treason for a free state to do the same thing; that there is no power under the Constitution to build a national railroad, but ample power to employ the Army and Navy of the country to catch fugitive slaves, and prevent the settlement of the territories of the nation by Non-Slaveholders; and last of all, that no democrat should hesitate to follow his party-leaders. We have been so successful in inculcating these principles, that many of the People really think them to be the code of genuine democracy. You perceive, however, that they substantially amount to this, that *fidelity and devotion to Slavery have become the one thing needful in American politics.*

Well, we were lately carrying into practice some of the more fruitful of these principles, in Kansas. We stole the territory from the People by act of Congress. We set loose the Slaveholders of an adjoining state on the residents there, and hau over-run and effectually subdued them, as we thought, though not indeed without some violence and occasional murders. The citizens of the territory made some resistance, it is true; still, our cause was advancing prosperously, and we bid fair to have the whole nation to back us. But in the full tide of our success, that fanatical Senator unveiled our proceedings, and let out the *great secret*, that the Slaveholders wished not only to possess black slaves, but to be masters of all the People likewise. It was an offense not to be forgiven. We who had been long in the service of the Slave Power as confirmed democrats, had always been careful not to blab the secret of its aims. Our offices and bread depend on our keeping it. But this insolent talker, who sits in Congress without asking any favors of the Slave Power, spoke the thing right out. Of course, we were obliged to punish him for vengeance, and also to prevent any such free speaking hereafter. So we did punish him. Two democratic Slaveholders inflicted on him a deserved chastisement, from which if he were to die, it would be all right. It is nothing more than has already been suffered by many a non-slaveholding citizen of Kansas. We modern democrats do not die for liberty, as our fathers did; we prefer rather to inflict death on those who love liberty too well.

The reason, then, of that penal infliction on the Senator was, that he revealed too plainly the doings of the Slave Power. For that Power, ruling Congress through the Democracy, took the matter in hand, and by first suggesting, and afterwards approving of the punishment of the Senator, has pretty thoroughly suppressed, as we think, all free speech in Congress for some time.

But scenes similar to the beating of the Senator may still occasionally occur. Our slaveholding masters are very chivalrous characters, and they do not readily tolerate any dissent from their own opinions. So it can not be known, with certainty, what slight grounds they may find for cudgeling the northern representatives. It behooves these gentlemen to walk softly, and not talk too much of liberty in Congress. We of the Democracy never open our lips in favor of freedom there. We know our place—for we are cudgeled in ways the People little dream of. The only thing unpleasant, however, to us—the better sort of democrats who are engaged in the service of the Slave Power—is, that past favors are apt to be forgotten. My own deserts have been overlooked in a manner little expected. But I hate to speak of the subject. I console myself with the reflection, that if I cannot soar very high hereafter, I can still continue to crawl.

You have another consolation, said the Alien. It is, that you are sacrificed in the support of those great democratic principles which you enunciated to me.

Oh, said the Magistrate, it is only the Slaveholders who derive any consolation, now-a-days, from the support of democratic principles.

DEMOCRATIC STATUTE IN FORCE IN KANSAS, JULY 4, 1856.

Be it enacted by the Governor and Legislative Assembly of the Territory of Kansas, as follows:

SECTION 1.—That every person, bond or free, who shall be convicted of actually raising a rebellion or insurrection of slaves, free negroes, or mulattoes, in this Territory, shall suffer death.

SEC. 2. Every free person who shall aid or assist in any rebellion or insurrection of slaves, free negroes, or mulattoes, or shall furnish arms, or do any overt act in furtherance of such rebellion or insurrection, shall suffer death.

SEC. 3. If any free person shall, by speaking, writing, or printing, advise, persuade, or induce any slaves to rebel, conspire against or murder any citizen of this Territory, or shall bring into print, write, publish, or circulate, or cause to be brought into, printed, written, published, or circulated, or shall knowingly aid or assist in the bringing into, printing, writing, publishing, or circulating, in this Territory, any book, paper, magazine, pamphlet or circular, for the purpose of exciting insurrection, rebellion, revolt, or conspiracy on the part of the slaves, free negroes or mulattoes, against the citizens of the Territory or any part of them, such person shall be guilty of felony, and suffer death.

SEC. 4. If any person shall entice, decoy, or carry away out of this Territory any slave belonging to another, with intent to deprive the owner thereof of the services of such slave, or with intent to effect or procure the freedom of such slave, he shall be adjudged guilty of grand larceny, and, on conviction thereof, shall suffer death, or be imprisoned at hard labor for not less than ten years.

SEC. 5. If any person shall aid or assist in enticing, decoying, or persuading, or carrying away, or sending out of this Territory any slave belonging to another with intent to procure or effect the freedom of such slave, or with intent to deprive the owner thereof of the services of such slave, he shall be adjudged guilty of grand larceny, and, on conviction thereof, shall suffer death, or be imprisoned at hard labor for not less than ten years.

SEC. 6. If any person shall entice, decoy, or carry away out of any State or other Territory of the United States any slave belonging to another, with intent to procure or effect the freedom of such slave, or to deprive the owners thereof of the services of such slave, and shall bring such slave into this Territory, he shall be adjudged guilty of grand larceny, in the same manner as if such slave had been enticed, decoyed, or carried away out of this Territory, and in such case the larceny may be charged to have been committed in any county of this Territory into or through which such slave shall have been brought by such person, and, on conviction thereof, the person offending shall suffer death, or be imprisoned at hard labor for not less than ten years.

SEC. 7. If any person shall entice, persuade or induce any slave to escape from the service of his master or owner in this Territory, or shall aid or assist any slave in escaping from the service of his master or owner, or shall aid, assist, harbor or conceal any slave who may have escaped from the service of his master or owner, shall be deemed guilty of felony, and punished by imprisonment at hard labor for a term of not less than five years.

SEC. 8. If any person in this Territory shall aid or assist, harbor or conceal any slave who has escaped from the service of his master or owner, in another State or Territory, such person shall be punished in like manner as if such slave had escaped from the service of his master or owner in this Territory.

SEC. 9. If any person shall resist any officer while attempting to arrest any slave that may have escaped from the service of his master or owner, or shall rescue such slave when in custody of any officer or other person, or shall entice, persuade, aid or assist such slave to escape from the custody of any officer or other person who may have such slave in custody, whether such slave have escaped from the service of his master or owner in this Territory, or in any other State or Territory, the person so offending shall be guilty of felony, and punished by imprisonment at hard labor for a term of not less than two years.

SEC. 10. If any marshal, sheriff, or constable, or the deputy of any such officer, shall, when required by any person, refuse to aid or assist in the arrest and capture of any slave that may have escaped from the service of his master or owner, whether such slave shall have escaped from his master or owner in this Territory, or any State or other Territory, such officer shall be fined in a sum of not less than one hundred nor more than five hundred dollars.

SEC. 11. If any person print, write, introduce into,

publish or circulate, or cause to be brought into, printed, written, published and circulated, or shall knowingly aid or assist in bringing into, printing, publishing or circulating within this Territory, any book, paper, pamphlet, magazine, handbill or circular, containing any statements, arguments, opinions, sentiments, doctrine, advice or inuendo, calculated to produce a disorderly, dangerous or rebellious disaffection among the slaves in this Territory, or to induce such slaves to escape from the service of their masters, or resist their authority, he shall be guilty of felony, and be punished by imprisonment and hard labor for a term not less than five years.

SEC. 12. If any free person, by speaking or by writing, assert or maintain that persons have not the right to hold slaves in this Territory, or shall introduce into this Territory, print, publish, write, circulate, or cause to be introduced into this Territory, written, printed, published or circulated in this Territory, any book, paper, magazine, pamphlet or circular containing any denial of the right of persons to hold slaves in this Territory, such person shall be deemed guilty of felony, and punished by imprisonment at hard labor for a term of not less than two years.

SEC. 13. No person who is conscientiously opposed to holding slaves, or who does not admit the right to hold slaves in this Territory, shall sit as a juror on the trial of any prosecution for any violation of any of the sections of this act.

This act to take effect and be in force from and after the fifteenth day of September, A. D. 1855.

www.ingramcontent.com/pod-product-compliance
Lightning Source LLC
LaVergne TN
LVHW020214110826
845151LV00003B/717
9781425533441